OPEN EYES, HAPPY HEART

A Story of Healing from Sexual Abuse and Childhood Trafficking

Carolyn Thompson

Open Eyes, Happy Heart Copyright © 2020 by Carolyn Thompson
Published in Little Rock, Arkansas, United States. All rights reserved.
ISBN 978-1-7354401-1-8
Library of Congress Control Number: 2020916150

re|engage™ Lesson 5 material paraphrased with permission from:
Watermark Community Church
7540 LBJ Fwy, Dallas TX 75251
www.watermarkresources.com

Definition of hosos taken from:
THAYER'S GREEK LEXICON, Electronic Database.
Copyright © 2002, 2003, 2006, 2011 by Biblesoft, Inc.
All rights reserved. Used by permission. BibleSoft.com

As noted, Scripture quotations are taken from:

The Holy Bible, Berean Study Bible, BSB
Copyright ©2016, 2018 by Bible Hub
Used by Permission. All Rights Reserved Worldwide.

The Holy Bible, New International Version® NIV®
Copyright © 1973 1978 1984 2011 by Biblica, Inc. TM
Used by permission. All rights reserved worldwide.

Scripture quotations marked (TLB) are taken from The Living Bible copyright © 1971. Used by permission of Tyndale House Publishers, a Division of Tyndale House Ministries, Carol Stream, Illinois 60188. All rights reserved.

No part of this publication may be reproduced, stored in a retrieval system, or transmitted in any form or by any means—electronic, mechanical, photocopy, recording, or any other—without the prior permission of the author. Any Internet addresses (websites, blogs, etc.) and telephone numbers in this book are offered as a resource. The author does not vouch for the continued validity of the resources for the life of this book.

Requests for information should be addressed to:
cthompson@openeyeshappyheart.com.
Connect on Social Media: @opneyeshppyhart on Instagram and Facebook

DEDICATION

To my mom,
who encouraged me to do whatever
I needed to do in order to heal.

To my friend Shannon,
for pointing me to God multiple times a day
when the fear was bad.

To my husband Will,
for bringing joy and light into
the darkest parts of my journey

Thank you for loving me so well

TABLE OF CONTENTS

◆◆◆

FOREWORD: LIVING IN VICTORY	i
by Greg Kirksey, Teaching Pastor, The Church at Rock Creek	
AN OPEN LETTER TO WOMEN'S MINISTRY LEADERS	iii
by Shannon Calhoun, Women's Ministry Director,	
The Church at Rock Creek	
AUTHOR'S INTRODUCTION: HIDDEN IN PLAIN SIGHT	v
PART ONE: INVITATION TO THE VALLEY	
Chapter 1 The Beginning and the End	1
Chapter 2 Seen and Unseen	10
Chapter 3 Who Do You Say I Am	21
PART TWO: THE GOOD SHEPHERD	
Chapter 4 The Path	35
Chapter 5 Fear Not	46
Chapter 6 Comfort	56
PART THREE: I SHALL NOT WANT	
Chapter 7 The Table Prepared	67
Chapter 8 Overflow	76
Chapter 9 Goodness and Mercy	83
AUTHOR'S CONCLUSION: LETTER TO MY DAD	92
AFTERWORD: ON FORGIVENESS AND FREEDOM	94
by Charles Speer, Paul and Silas Prison Ministries	
AUTHOR'S THANK YOU	95
CHAPTER DISCUSSION QUESTIONS	97
RESOURCES	
Celebrate Recovery	106
Partners Against Trafficking Humans	107
The Church At Rock Creek	108

FOREWORD: LIVING IN VICTORY BY PASTOR GREG KIRKSEY

◆◆◆

For more than twenty-five years I have found myself used by God again and again to help people navigate the rough and rocky trail of grief. It can be an especially difficult journey when travelled alone. Thus, it has been my honor and privilege to walk alongside many whose hearts have been crushed.

God equipped me for this sensitive ministry through a series of numerous trials and personal losses in my own life. My own painful journey has enabled me to win the trust of those facing heartbreaking grief. By battling through my own dark days of agony, I am viewed as a fellow struggler, and my message of comfort and hope is given credibility as one who understands their pain.

However, the unthinkable pain Carolyn Thompson experienced as a girl growing up is something I can neither understand nor fathom. Unfortunately, there are many who can. If you are a victim of sexual abuse or human trafficking it is not an accident that you have picked up this book. Carolyn understands your agony, and as a victim of repeated sexual abuse herself she can relate to the trauma and pain that tortures your every step. Recovering from abuse is never easy but having someone who understands your pain to walk alongside you is a gift you must not turn down.

In this book Carolyn details her remarkable journey that offers hope. While Carolyn may be a victim of sexual abuse, she has chosen not to live like one.

It is easy for 'survivors' to feel like victims doomed to live isolated and lonely lives in the shadows, haunted by their painful pasts. This of course is not living at all. So, God sent His Son Jesus to earth to rescue and redeem us, and through His grace enables you to do the unthinkable, to live as a victor not a victim.

I've never personally known anyone who exemplifies this

miraculous transformation like Carolyn. By God's amazing grace He has enabled her to emerge from her personal nightmare with a story of vibrant hope so wonderful that only God could have written this story.

My hope is that by reading this book, you will let the God of grace Who rescued Carolyn from the darkness of her sexual abuse to change your life too.

Greg Kirksey
Teaching Pastor
The Church at Rock Creek
11500 W 36th Street Little Rock, AR 72211
churchatrockcreek.com

AN OPEN LETTER TO WOMEN'S MINISTRY LEADERS BY SHANNON CALHOUN

◆◆◆

July 16, 2020

Taboo topics. Uncomfortable, touchy, real life stuff. Women's Ministry leaders, we have to go there.

We'd love not to have to go there, pretending such evil doesn't exist. The truth is, however, it does exist and we cannot continue to sleep through it. Horrific abuse is happening all around us. The enemy is on the prowl and he is devouring.

So, what if we talked about sex trafficking in church?

Carolyn and I meet for prayer on Wednesdays. I asked her to join me in praying my family through a difficult time. What I didn't know is that Carolyn would then choose to begin sharing her story with me. Carolyn knew it was time, because in sharing this story, she could provide real understanding and encouragement that can only come from someone who has walked a relatable path.

While the story of my family situation and hers is very different, God was able to use Carolyn's story to speak life into ours because of her obedience to Him. I've had the honor of seeing my friend's continued obedience to our Heavenly Father and the way He has so obviously led her every step. I've seen the power of the Holy Spirit, grace, and forgiveness pour out of Carolyn where from a worldly perspective it would only make sense to see a victim, and anger, and shame.

So a better question is: What if we DON'T talk about sex trafficking in church? What then? Do we continue to remain asleep? Do we leave it outside the house of our community of believers and hope for the best? Wouldn't the devil be so satisfied if we shied away from talking? He wants to kill, steal, and destroy. He wants it to remain in the dark.

Maybe someone is waiting on this conversation to know that she will be loved even if someone knows her past. Maybe she is waiting to hear someone say she is not alone in the abuse she suffered. Maybe she is waiting on the church to say 'even that' is not beyond our Father's miraculous healing, even for her.

She is deeply loved by the Father and you just might be the lifeline that sustains her until she knows her worth in Him. You might help her to open the door to freedom that she never understood was there. It's scary, but you can listen and love and pray. You can walk alongside her as she gets the help she needs, and you can celebrate together as you see God do what only He can.

Better together.
(Ecclesiastes 4:9-10)

Shannon Calhoun
Women's Ministry Director
The Church at Rock Creek
11500 W 36th Street
Little Rock, AR 72211
churchatrockcreek.com

AUTHOR'S INTRODUCTION: HIDDEN IN PLAIN SIGHT

"Call to Me and I will answer and show you great and unsearchable things you do not know." Jeremiah 33:3 BSB

A lot of survivors talk about how they got their voices taken away and spent years struggling to find them. And that's true and important. But I'm here to tell you about how I got my sight taken away and spent years struggling to find it. And beyond that, I'm here to tell you about how the world has had its sight taken away, and the Lord wants to give it back.

The two biggest commandments God gave us were to love Him and to love our neighbors as ourselves. But can we love God if we can't see who He truly is? Or love ourselves, if we can't grasp how God sees us? Or love our neighbors the way God was actually describing?

Would you like to see the world as God intended?

The most terrible thing that happened to me through the years of childhood abuse I suffered wasn't the damage it did to my physical being or to my mind. It was the damage it did to my soul. The worst thing that happened was that the eyes of my heart were blinded.

This book is the story of how God healed the eyes of my heart. And it's an invitation from Him to you to do the same in your life.

PART ONE: INVITATION TO THE VALLEY

CHAPTER ONE:
THE BEGINNING AND THE END

"He has made everything beautiful in its time. He has also set eternity in the hearts of men, yet they cannot fathom the work that god has done from beginning to end." Ecclesiastes 3:11 BSB

◆◆◆

My story begins near the end of what has been my life so far. It will take you on a journey through a valley which the Lord ordered me to enter and I tried to run away from instead. My valley story is messy, painful, humbling, and—to me at least—incredibly beautiful because of what God did there and how it changed everything.

In December of 2018, I thought my life was manageable. I was serving in volunteer ministry and had just finished improving my marriage through a wonderful re|engage course. But the truth was I was already wandering in the wilderness. My sense of purpose was adrift. I had finished homeschooling, entered the empty nest phase, and had no clear vision for what to do with the rest of my life.

At the end of Christmas vacation in Oklahoma with my husband's family, I slipped away, pulled out my iPhone, and watched a Sunday service broadcast online from my home church, the Church at Rock Creek in Little Rock, Arkansas.

The message was about happiness, of all things: how the church had an artificial distinction between the words "happiness" and "joy". Our Teaching Pastor Greg Kirksey shared that there was no scriptural, linguistic or historical basis for making that distinction: that in fact, the Bible was filled with references to happiness, because the primary Hebrew and Greek words for "blessed" and "happy" were the same words. Therefore God was interested in our happiness, just not the worldly version that involved no suffering. God's version of happiness was holy.

Greg used Psalm 1 to make a case for what Christ-centered

happiness looked like vs. self-centered happiness. Christ-centered happiness involved keeping our distance from the world (being in it, but not of it); keeping our delight in the Word of God; and keeping our devotion to the Work of God. So the road to a Happy New Year was paved with three habits: scheduling our time wisely, studying our Bibles regularly, and serving the Lord unselfishly.

I knew that I wasn't happy. And I thought I knew what my biggest area of unhappiness was. The perplexing thing was that I thought I was regularly practicing the habits that Greg listed.

I decided I'd make "happiness" my focus for 2019 and see if I could figure out what was out of alignment. I had absolutely no idea what I was getting into—it turned my world upside down. But it's a decision I'm profoundly grateful that I made.

While I was still in Oklahoma, I had gotten a text from my friend Samantha about her husband, my friend Travis. Travis had suffered a bad bicycle accident. After a complicated surgery in early January, he ended up with a plate and screws to rebuild his shattered left collarbone, and 2 plates and screws in his right hand. With neither arm functioning, he was temporarily helpless.

By the middle of January, Travis was doing well enough to have visitors at home. I went to see him, and of course asked all about the wreck. He said that he and a friend, both experienced riders, had gone to check out the new Northwood MTP Trail system in Hot Springs, AR. They were having fun but being cautious to examine unfamiliar terrain as they went. Travis said that when he scoped out a Black Diamond trail they were about to ride, he looked long and hard at the last big gap they were going to jump. It was really wide. He decided that if he hit the jumps preceding that one perfectly—was in the zone—he'd go for that last jump. Otherwise, he wouldn't.

He did hit those jumps perfectly as he rode down the trail. He was feeling secure as he went for the last one. It was only after he launched into the air that he realized it was all going wrong, and that he was going to need to ditch his bike before hitting the other side. Ditching the bike was better than hitting, but it still left him lying broken on the ground, unable to get up unaided or even to unclip his own helmet.

Travis and I sat for a long while and had a deep conversation about what it was like to have your "normal" shattered—to go from independent and doing your own thing to needing to rely on God and other people just to get through everyday tasks. It could have been a downer of a conversation, but it wasn't: it was exactly the opposite. We were focused on the amazing and eye-opening things God was doing in the middle of humbling circumstances. Travis had a lot to share with me from just the few weeks of healing he had already been through—and he knew he had a long journey still ahead of him.

As we talked, I mentioned to Travis that I was going to pursue "happiness" as my goal for 2019. I didn't share much, just that it seemed that God wanted to do something different with my family circumstances to achieve that goal, and it was likely to be hard. Travis gave a short laugh and warned me that praying for happiness could be dangerous, like praying for patience—an invitation to a whole bunch of testing. He also said that family change could be hard. But he finished by saying that hard things were often worth doing. It was a great visit, and we both parted encouraged.

There was a reason I wasn't more forthcoming with Travis about my family situation. I had a secret which my husband knew, but which the rest of my daily world did not: that my dad had sexually abused me as a child.

As an adult I had forgiven my dad, even before I came to Christ. And to all appearances, though not in words, my dad was sorry for everything that he had done. He had gone to great lengths to try and be a better father. When I forgave him back in 1995, we resumed a relationship, though not a close one.

Then, in 2012, three things happened: my dad had an accident which injured his brain and could have killed or permanently disabled him (but didn't, thank God); he chose to stay sober after he recovered; and I altered my boundaries and really rebuilt our relationship. I was praying to get the gospel in front of him and help him find Jesus like I had. I was afraid of what would happen to him if he didn't: he was a confirmed Christ-denier. So I believed it was worth the moderate worsening of my PTSD symptoms to make the effort.

And it did make my PTSD symptoms worse. For seven years, while I built relationship and looked for opportunities to share my faith, I suffered more sleep problems, appetite problems, recurring depression and anxiety. And my panic and hyperawareness problems, especially at night, ranged from annoying to occasionally debilitating.

I hadn't fully trusted or understood who God was when He saved me. And I still hadn't wholly embraced the new identity He had given me. Blind to the riches before me, I suffered in silence and did my best to hide my struggle. I plunged forward, not seeking help, until the day I prayed for happiness. And God was ready for that moment—even though He knew it meant I would need to have an unexpected crash of my own.

I had done my very best to forget an additional part of my childhood, lumping it under "sexual abuse" and never discussing it with anyone—not even my husband. I was hiding from the reality that my dad hadn't just sexually abused me himself but had also trafficked me during my elementary school years.

The reality of having been trafficked was beyond my capacity to deal with alone; and I wasn't planning to share it with another soul. This left me fighting an endless battle to block it out and shove it down into the deepest recesses of my brain.

I did everything possible to pretend either that it didn't matter, because I'd forgiven my dad; or that it didn't affect me in any way, which wasn't true; or even that it never happened at all. My internal "truth" was whatever would help keep me going at any given time. The repressed memory problems inherent in PTSD fueled this and kept me functioning in my dysfunction for many years. But it was exhausting.

Are you endlessly battling something in your past?

After I started focusing on happiness, I had moments of awareness that God was shepherding me toward dealing with exactly what I was trying so hard to avoid. But the glimpses were so overwhelming to me that I would "know" and then "not know" where we were headed.

On February 9, 2019, when we streamed the second day of the IF:Gathering at Rock Creek, I'd had a complete meltdown over what God had put in front of me. During the IJM presentation about child sex trafficking in Cambodia I had panicked and desperately wanted to run. But I was also too terrified to move. I was afraid that if I got up and exited the event, people would somehow know what my history was. The irrational fear was intense. It was only with enormous effort that I was able to get up and leave for the ladies' room.

When I got there, I hid in a stall, hyperventilated, tried not to throw up, and was generally miserable. I wanted to pound on the metal stall walls. I wanted to ball up on the floor and sob. I did neither. Instead I froze there, my face buried in my hands.

Eventually enough time passed that I became worried

someone would check on me to see if I was okay—attention I didn't want either. So I slowed my breathing as best I could, got some water from the fountain, and headed back to the Community Room.

Thankfully, the IJM presentation was over, and no one had been looking for me. Trembling, I sat and wrote these words in my event journal, praying no friend would look over my shoulder:

IJM / Cambodia
- I feel terrible guilt that I am not freeing children from the kind of abuse I suffered.
- I want to be free from the abuse being my life.
- My own pain from what I've been through is unresolved.
- I have/Have I moved forward?
- I don't feel called to it. God has not asked.
- Why do I feel guilty?

Temporarily unburdened, I shut the journal. Then PTSD blocked out the experience, allowing me to go back to my "normal" life—more or less. But the words are there in my February 9 notes—in my own handwriting—undeniable. I was shocked to discover them as I pulled material together for this book. I "forgot" the entire experience you just read about until I rediscovered what I had written.

It wasn't until May, after God spent a whole lot more time working on me, that He finally encouraged me to look at the problem of unhappiness and have an actual conversation with Him about where we were going. It started on Mother's Day with another sermon, this one from our Senior Pastor Mark Evans.

I was at home sick and joined the online stream from Rock Creek late. Mark was already launching into his first point. As I listened to the sermon, "Showing Mercy to Family," I was increasingly uncomfortable.

I was pretty certain I had been merciful to my dad. I thought I had, as Mark phrased it, "ignored the irritations" (*"Love is not irritable or easily angered." 1 Cor 13:5 NIV*). I thought I had "done good when it wasn't deserved" (*"Love keeps no record of wrongs." 1 Cor 13:5b NIV*). I was sure I had "let go of past hurts", and "believed God was at work" in my dad's life (*"Love is not rude. Love does not demand its own way. It is not irritable or touchy. It does not hold grudges. Love always trusts, love is always hopeful, and love always perseveres through whatever comes." 1 Cor 13:5 TLB*). What was the problem?

I wondered about it enough that that I wrote the three action items for "Showing Mercy to Family" in dry erase marker on my bathroom mirror for further reflection:
1. Say no when needed;
2. Respond, don't react; and
3. Learn to love in freedom, not guilt.

I knew my swirling feelings included guilt, but I couldn't figure out why.

Monday I was still unsettled, and still sick. I didn't get a lot done. Then, about 9 PM, I got a text from my dad that stopped me cold. It was a simple message. All it said was "I remember you were a very interesting and clever little kid. I wish I had taken notes. You said lots of neat things."

My dad texted me pretty frequently. He usually wrote about relatives and neighbors. This text, though, I had a strange reaction to: I went numb. I felt the world recede around me and I couldn't breathe. I had no idea why. I stared at the words for several minutes. Then I texted him what seemed like an appropriate response: a heart emoji and a hug emoji. I tried to recover and finish the conversation normally. Afterwards I found myself pacing back and forth through the upstairs rooms, unable to sit still.

The evening grew more surreal a half hour later when my neighbor B. W., a great Christian friend and mentor to me, got taken away to the hospital with chest pains and very high blood pressure. I barely slept that night. I had no doubt about where he would go if he died, but I wasn't ready for him to go anywhere.

I called and talked to B.W. the next morning—he was in ICU while they looked at his heart and got his blood pressure down—and then I took care of my own illness, visiting my doctor and getting antibiotics for strep. I got home shortly before noon.

My husband had left his home office to lead a men's bible study at church. So I was alone.

My father's text from the previous night was still inexplicably bugging me. It circled through my head again and again. I walked upstairs to try and shake it off. I ended up in front of that mirror where I'd listed those action steps. I read through them several times, slowly.

Suddenly the numbness broke. I found I had brought my fists down on the counter, spun and punched the door, and kicked the bathroom cabinet multiple times.

To say this was abnormal would be an understatement. I couldn't figure out what was happening. I started yelling at God. What, I asked Him, WAS this? WHAT was wrong? Wasn't I doing everything He wanted me to do in my life, seeking His Will, growing and serving? Why, especially, would He be allowing me to be in such incomprehensible turmoil when my focus word was HAPPY?

Do you both long for and dread major life change?

God answered those questions with what I definitely didn't want to hear: that the sermon had bothered me because I had buried my anger rather than dealing with it. I needed to get help. I needed to look directly at the trafficking (and other abuse I had never admitted) and gain a new perspective. He brought to my mind Psalm 23, telling me it was a promise:

"*The LORD is my shepherd; I shall not want.*
He makes me lie down in green pastures;
He leads me beside quiet waters.

He restores my soul; He guides me in the paths of righteousness for the sake of His name.
Even though I walk through the valley of the shadow of death, I will fear no evil, for You are with me;
Your rod and Your staff, they comfort me.
You prepare a table before me in the presence of my enemies. You anoint my head with oil; my cup overflows.
Surely goodness and mercy will follow me all the days of my life, and I will dwell in the house of the LORD forever."
(Psalm 23 BSB)

God said it was time to head into the valley to travel to green pastures. And He asked me, just like Jesus asked the man at the pool of Bethesda, "Do you want to get well?" (John 5:6b BSB).

CHAPTER TWO:
SEEN AND UNSEEN

"For our struggle is not against flesh and blood, but against the rulers, against the authorities, against the powers of this world's darkness, and against the spiritual forces of evil in the heavenly realms." Ephesians 6:12 BSB

◆◆◆

Generational sin is a real thing. So is spiritual warfare. The two are inextricably intertwined. The family is a high value target in the war the enemy is waging against God.

Generational sin doesn't mean that God holds the sins of one person against another; in fact, the Bible explicitly states that He does not: *"In those days, it will no longer be said: 'The fathers have eaten sour grapes, and the teeth of the children are set on edge.' Instead, each will die for his own iniquity. If anyone eats the sour grapes, his own teeth will be set on edge" (Jeremiah 31:29-30 BSB).*

Nevertheless, patterns and consequences of sin travel down generational lines. My own childhood abuse didn't spring out of thin air: rather it festered from previous evil waged against my flesh and blood by Hell itself.

Please understand: I am in no way saying my parents are blameless—no human beings are. Every last one of us is a sinner in need of grace *(Romans 3:23)*. But my parents are survivors of spiritual warfare and generational sin just as I am. God loves them deeply, and they deserve compassion *(1 John 4:19)*.

Has generational sin affected your family?

What I'm about to relate is based on things both of my parents have told me over many years. Some are stories they disclosed about their own pasts; others are stories they shared about each other. (It's all I have to go on; I obviously wasn't there myself.)

My father grew up in a home where love was mixed with pain and secret keeping. My grandpa's alcohol addiction, cruelty and insecurity took an enormous toll on the family. During the worst years, my dad was engaged in a daily battle both to help keep grandpa's drinking hidden from the outside world and to escape grandpa's anger himself. He has recounted stories of coming home from school and routinely unplugging the phone to prevent his dad from making drunken angry phone calls later in the evening. Other times Dad feared for his own safety. He still has pain over a terrifying road trip Grandpa took him on just because he wanted my dad to be the one to walk into the store and purchase cigarettes. (Grandpa didn't want anyone to see him staggering into the store, but he was fine with swerving all over the road driving there and back. It's a miracle no one was hurt or killed.) Beyond that, "discipline" wasn't applied in a predictable or constructive way: an out-of-control parent applies out-of-control punishment.

My grandma's behavior shaped my Dad's expectations of and feelings about women in negative ways. She helped hide her husband's drinking until the night it almost killed my dad; and in general she made it clear to my dad that earning her love was a race he was always losing to his younger sister. He never quite measured up.

This was hard to reconcile with everything my dad admired about his mom: how she basically raised her younger siblings; how she survived the Great Depression; and how she wouldn't let anything stop her from reaching goals she wanted to achieve (college education among them).

My dad loved his parents, but they both hurt him deeply. He grew up feeling terribly guilty about all the anger he felt.

My dad went to church as a child. He heard the Word of God

and rejected it. Hope wasn't a message he trusted: smart people expected the worst and were pleasantly surprised if something else happened.

Additional barriers against accepting the Word formed. He came of age at a time when sexual mores were being turned upside down and drug use was increasingly common. And he chose to go into political science as his field of study, where religious belief was viewed as a tool, not a reality.

Living apart from God's truth about love and redemption, it's not surprising that my dad turned to what was available to numb out while maintaining a front for the outside world. He created a life patterned after the way he had grown up, though the details were definitely different.

My mother, on the other hand, was raised in the church and came to Christ willingly. She was the oldest of six, one of whom died early of childhood illness. My maternal grandma went through major depression over that loss, while being simultaneously pregnant with her sixth child. Mom had to step up and take on an adult role in the household she didn't feel equal to carrying.

Economic conditions were very difficult. It bothered my mom greatly when she discovered her parents had married because she was conceived out of wedlock. She knew that they loved her, but the sense of responsibility and guilt for things outside of her control lingered. She married her high school sweetheart to escape home, but soon found herself young and divorced in a society where that was still unusual. She married my dad knowing he was a non-believer and she would be unequally yoked, but she loved him, and it looked like a better life. It caused her pain that her mother-in-law looked down on her for her background, but my mom was determined to make her new life work at all costs. There would be no more failure. It was hard though. She suffered from recurring anxiety and depression. These were the two broken people who came together and created me. I love them both with all of my heart, and I'm grateful that they did. I'm glad to be alive. But because of all the generational sin, the enemy had a playground readymade for my arrival.

One of the best early memories I have is a visual. It's of my brother. He was born—prematurely—when I was about two and half years old. He stayed in the hospital for a little while. I remember the first time I laid eyes on him at home. He looked right back at me. I didn't expect that. He was smaller than my dolls. His eyes were blue, and his skin was pink. I was amazed. I thought he was beautiful.

Mostly because my brother was a preemie, he took much longer to start sleeping through the night than other babies. My mom was constantly exhausted.

One of the worst early memories I have is of my dad deciding to "help" my mom when I was three—unbeknownst to her—by teaching me not to call out for attention during the night. He did that by holding a pillow over my face when he tucked me in, suffocating me just long enough to scare me.

My dad was like two people. Substance abuse factored in, as did his own childhood, but I didn't know any of that at the time. I just knew that he alternately terrified me and doted on me during my preschool years. In front of people he'd relate at length all the "neat" things I was learning to do and say. Alone he still might compliment me—much like he did in the text that inexplicably bugged me later—but he was just as likely to scream at me for upsetting his drink or "accidentally" kick me to teach me not to be underfoot. He also liked to "share" sips from his drinks. It made me sleepy. I'm sure it kept me quiet when he did it. Noise and activity around my dad have always been problems for him.

I couldn't have articulated it at that age, but I was starting to feel like two people myself. One was smart, pretty, a clever little kid who did and said "neat" things—and the other was a complete annoyance, worthless, and always in need of correction. The mixed messages were confusing and clouded my sense of identity. I tried to cling to the compliments—my mom echoed them, so I hoped they were true. But the competing message was difficult to see past.

When my parents tell stories about this time period, my mom will remark on how all they had to do was look at me if I did something wrong and I would start crying. There was no need for discipline. My dad will agree and talk about what

Does your sense of value depend on how others see you?

a tender heart I had. He leaves out the fact that there had been plenty of "discipline".

I know the enemy did horrible damage to my dad in his own childhood, and he hasn't had Jesus in his life to heal him. Today, watching my dad hide from the past and try to work out his own redemption, my heart breaks. I wish he knew how much joy and peace would come from putting that heavy burden into the hands of Christ. The forgiveness I've given my dad can't provide the type of freedom he could be experiencing.

The year my baby sister was born, my dad got a new job and we moved from Illinois to Arkansas. At first, I was excited about the move. My mom likes to relate the story of me telling the lady at the Arkansas Welcome Center how I was going to learn to talk "just like her!" My mom says the lady was highly amused.

I remember wandering all over the new house with my little brother, who was almost three. We explored everything. We were especially intrigued by the storage closet under the stairs—we thought it was spooky—and by how weird it was going to be for our rooms to be so far apart.

The new house was a split level. Stairs led down from the entryway to two bedrooms: one medium-sized and the other a master suite. Upstairs from the entryway were the living room, dining room, kitchen, three bedrooms, and a second full bath. There was an additional half bath attached to the largest bedroom.

My parents were going to take the largest bedroom upstairs. My brother and sister would be in the two rooms across the hall from them. My dad's office would fill the medium-sized downstairs room, and I would be put in the master suite next to it. I was told that I was a big enough girl to handle the isolation, and my mom needed to be close to the baby. I wasn't crazy about being alone, but I was starting kindergarten soon and wanted to be thought of as a big girl.

My new bedroom was a large, cold room with bright red carpet. Because the room was mostly underground, it was dark—there was just one small window near my new ceiling. The attached bathroom was wallpapered with giant red velvet flowers on a white background. None of it was what you'd call pretty.

My mom decorated the bedroom in a patriotic theme to make me like it better, and at first, I did. She even made a cute smiley face cover for the vent over my bed, so the room wasn't so freezing cold. But because that was the room where my dad started sexually abusing me, nothing could ever make it a really good place.

There was often shouting and arguing in our new house. We were not a happy family. I don't remember what most of it was about, but I do remember wanting people to feel better.

I got terrible headaches and tension over everyday life. To "help" me, my dad started giving me "massage therapy" which progressed from appropriate to inappropriate touch pretty swiftly. It eventually culminated in rape.

It was impossible to sort out—my father's "help" and all the horrible feelings that resulted. The enemy was at work damaging my view that a father was someone who would provide good help when I needed it.

Do you avoid asking for help that you need?

◆◆◆

My desire to fix the volatile situation at home meant I also became driven to help all the adults around me feel better.

One schoolteacher told my mom about it, praising me for my compassion in noticing her bad day and taking time to comfort her. I took this relayed praise to heart, and "comforter" became part of my "good" identity.

But my dad exploited that too. He'd tell me sad stories, cry, break my heart for him, and then make himself feel better in ways that no father ever should. Afterwards he would tell me how smart, beautiful, and special I was—everything my broken heart wanted to believe combined with everything that made me want to curl up and die.

That same dynamic played out in some of the trafficking. I remember asking my dad once why we were on the way to see a particular man, and my dad telling me that the man was sad because his wife was in the hospital. The man was lonely. He just needed someone to make him feel better. I wanted to help and be a "good girl", didn't I? The enemy was at work perverting my view of myself as someone who had love worth offering to others.

Every form of manipulation that my dad used corrupted my sense of identity in some way, but none so much as abusing my desire to make him proud. Once he told me that he wanted to "show off his wonderful daughter" so I should dress up and be sweet to a man who was about to visit.

During the visit, dad called me into the kitchen and gave me juice I didn't suspect was drugged. I fell asleep in a living room chair in broad daylight and woke up hours later, unclothed in my own bed, staring at my stuffed animals and coloring books. My mom and siblings had been in the house, oblivious to my situation. Dad had simply carried his sleeping daughter downstairs to tuck her in like a good father, his friend in tow. Then they hung out in his office. That was what my mom thought happened. I know because I asked after I got dressed and went upstairs.

Do you hide behind walls in your relationships?

It was a new reality that I could be trafficked in my own home, not just out somewhere. It was a much more difficult reality to grasp. The enemy was at work eroding my view of myself as valuable—so many things declared me worthless.

❖❖❖

Do you trust love when it's offered to you?

The more my sense of identity and morality was confused, the less manipulating my dad needed to do to get what he wanted. But he continued manipulating me. And drugging me.

The combination of manipulation, drugs and trafficking turned my childhood into a living nightmare.

The craziest part was that my ordinary childhood life continued right alongside my nightmare. I still went to school. I still went to church with my mom. I even played with neighborhood children and went to Girl Scouts—at least until my anger and increasing PTSD symptoms made it too difficult to connect with my peers. Then library books became my refuge. The trafficking eventually stopped for reasons I'm not willing to discuss publicly. But the sexual abuse continued longer, and my home life was miserable.

◆◆◆

When I was 12, I tried to run away. From my perspective, it was something I just suddenly did. With the severity of the PTSD problems I was having at the time though, it's more likely that something had happened I don't remember. What I do remember is that I didn't pack a bag; I didn't pack food; I didn't even have a destination in mind. I just knew I had to get out immediately.

I had been moved upstairs by that point, and my parents had taken the master suite downstairs. So I had a window in my bedroom that opened at ground level into the backyard.

Feeling like I was in another world, I walked over and shut the bedroom door as silently as possible. Then I put on my jacket, grabbed the only ten dollars I had, and slid open the window.

As I popped out the screen and lowered it to the ground, I was listening so hard for any change in sound from down the hall, I even stopped breathing. But all I heard was ordinary living room noise—television and muffled conversation. No one was coming.

I climbed out the open window and into the backyard. My mouth was completely dry. My teeth were chattering. But my feet were on the ground. So I slid the window closed as quietly as I could and headed down the slope to the backyard gate.

It was twilight, the sun setting fast behind the trees, as I stepped onto the driveway. I started down the hill, slowly at first, afraid a neighbor might be out and notice me. When I saw that I was alone, I let gravity start pulling me until eventually I was running full speed downhill toward the bottom end of our street. I reached the stop sign, turned right, and finally stood at a busy intersection—a literal crossroads. I paused. I had no clue what to do next.

As I considered taking the small amount of cash I had and getting fries at the nearby fast food restaurant, God interrupted me.

If you've ever wondered if God communicates with non-followers—and you really shouldn't wonder if you've read your Bible (*Genesis 41, Numbers 22:12, Daniel 4*)—I can confirm for you that He definitely does. I was in no way living for Christ at that point in my life, though I had been educated about Him at my mom's church and even professed to believe.

I had really wanted to follow Christ. I particularly loved the book of Luke. But I had a problem with God—I couldn't get past the whole "loving Father" concept.

That evening, as I stood at the crossroads, the experience of God interrupting me both solidified His reality and made it even harder for me to understand who He was. Because what He told me—not audibly but just as real as if He had spoken out loud—was, "Go home."

I was dumbfounded. If there was truly a God, and apparently there was, surely He wouldn't send me back THERE? Not when I had just gotten free?

"Go home," He repeated. "I can't! I can't!" I wailed at Him. "Go home," He said. "This is not your path."

It was too much for me. I sobbed, turned around, and went back the way I had come, all the way up the hill. I re-entered the backyard, re-entered the house, and re-entered everything.

I lived out my teen years, did well in high school despite everything, earned a scholarship and left home for college. But I found it impossible to believe that God loved me. And I certainly didn't love Him. I wanted Him not to exist.

When I got older, it did occur to me that my future on the streets would have been terrible—much like the proverbial jumping out of the frying pan and into the fire. And it did make sense that God would disallow that. But it didn't answer the bigger questions of why He would allow my situation to exist in the first place, or why He would send me back into it rather than removing me to safety.

Do you have any "WHY" questions about your past?

The enemy had done tremendous damage to me during my childhood. So much so that later, when I did come to Christ, I buried the "why" questions and pretended they didn't exist or didn't matter...like a lot of other abuse I had survived. That was the wrong perspective to take on very big questions about God's character. My Heavenly Father understood my brokenness but wouldn't allow me to continue like that forever. He loved me way too much.

CHAPTER THREE: WHO DO YOU SAY I AM

"God is not a man, that He should lie, or a son of man, that He should change His mind. Does He speak and not act? Does He promise and not fulfill?" Numbers 23:19 BSB

◆◆◆

On Tuesday, May 14, 2019, about noon, when God told me it was time to get well from ALL the abuse I'd been through—to stop lying and get help—I was not polite. I responded by yelling at Him some more.

I told Him that I had no intention of entering His "valley" and heading for mythical greener pastures. I told Him that I wanted my "normal" back. It didn't matter that I had been suffering—that I hadn't truly been happy. I wanted to function in my dysfunction like I'd been doing. I basically pointed at the fields I had been grazing in and insisted the grass was going to hold out forever.

Then I told God (which is ridiculous) who I was. I was a good wife, a good mom, a good ministry worker, and a good friend. And what He was telling me to do was going to strip all of that away from me, ruin my life, and basically kill me.

So, I told Him, the conversation was closed. (Like that was going to work.) I literally picked up my phone and started doing ordinary things like sending email and replying to texts. I was just going to get past this experience like every other unwanted thing that had ever happened to me. I was going to stonewall God. Except…

My neighbor B.W., who I loved, was still seriously ill. When I spoke to him at 6 PM, he told me that his doctors had scheduled a cardiac catheterization for the next day at 3 PM.

And I found myself telling him I would pray through the whole procedure for his safety, as well as praying that evening.

I realized that evening that I couldn't keep my promise. One of the things God created me to be was a prayer warrior, and I was well aware that to pray effectively, I needed to confess my sin, ask forgiveness, and align myself with God's will. So I knew I had a problem: because I really, really wanted my prayers for my neighbor to be effective—and I really, really didn't want to do those steps.

On Wednesday morning, still at home recovering from strep, still wrestling with God, I lay on the carpet of our home office and prayed. (My husband was working downtown, so the room was mine.)

This time, instead of yelling at God, I had a conversation with Him. I started by telling Him I was sorry. And then I told Him why I was struggling. (He knew, but I needed to say it.)

Do you define yourself through your roles?

The way I felt about myself terrified me. I had nagging feelings that I wasn't even a "real person" like everyone around me—I was just somehow "less". The relationships I had that connected me to others—"good wife", "good mom", "good ministry worker", "good friend"—without those, I was nothing. I was less than nothing. No matter how many times God told me otherwise, I would always lose the lesson. It would melt away under fire. At my core, I was convinced everyone would leave me if they knew my history—starting with my husband. And I'd already been through him leaving me once before.

I told God that my husband leaving me again couldn't possibly be His plan for my marriage after all that He had done to fix it. That's why I was so sure there was no happiness the direction He was telling me to go.

God responded by asking me who He was to me. I pulled up short.

"You're my Father. You created me, love me, and saved me through Your Son Jesus Christ."

He asked me if He had been good to me.

"Yes, You have. Many times over."

He asked me if I trusted Him with my life.

"You know I do—I chose Jesus."

He said that was true, but the question wasn't about the past—it was about the present. Not salvation but sanctification.

I thought. Hard. Did I mean what I said about following Christ? How often did I pray for the courage to do whatever God's will was? Often. These circumstances looked nothing like what I thought God's will could possibly be, but He was telling me that in fact, they were.

I took another look at the direction that God was pointing and tried to see a valley instead of a pit. I wasn't sure, even squinting, that I could bring it into focus.

But His history was rock solid. There had never been a point since I had started following Jesus where what God had wanted for me had turned out to be the wrong course of action. And there had been many times when what I thought was the better choice turned out to be wildly wrong.

I was still terrified. But I also thought about how much I loved my neighbor and wanted to pray for him. I had to decide what I believed—what was most important.

So I said, "Yes, God. I'll go get help. Please help my neighbor."

And I lay on the floor and prayed through the day, and through my neighbor's heart procedure. It turned out he had a blockage that was threatening a widowmaker. He could have died if God's hands hadn't been all over his care. Instead he was fine—his recovery was so fast and smooth that he was fishing on the White River several days later. It was amazing.

I was very grateful. And completely, 100% scared by the magnitude of what I'd agreed to do.

♦♦♦

I had meant that "yes" with my whole heart, but my flesh was paralyzed by fear. When I did nothing immediately to act on my "yes", God let my PTSD symptoms worsen. There was no way He was going to let me go back to my "normal". I couldn't eat; I couldn't sleep; and I had full-fledged flashbacks in the middle of night. I kept trying to come up with some way that I could go get therapy without telling my husband. There just wasn't one.

Do you avoid things that frighten you?

Because God has a sense of humor, my husband and I had tickets to Marriage Night at church that Friday (a stream of Dr. and Mrs. Leslie Parrot, Francis and Lisa Chan, and Comedian Michael Jr.). We were going to meet with friends from our Couples Life Group. I'm not even sure I can describe to you what it's like to go to a marriage event with your husband and other couples when you're afraid your marriage is about to end. The best I can do is to tell you that I felt like I had a hidden terminal illness.

My husband was so incredibly sweet and attentive the whole evening—complimenting me, holding my hand, whispering private jokes in my ear. I kept thinking how handsome and wonderful he was; how grateful I was God had put us back together; and how crazy it was to think that God would allow anything to break that apart. I thought about how much I loved Will, and how things had gone from good to amazing after the re|engage course the previous fall. Being at that Marriage Night made me think about who we were—a lot.

◆◆◆

My husband Will and I are wildly different from the two people we were when we met and started dating in New Orleans back in 1991. As we got to know each other then, I learned that he had a tough family history of his own—nothing on the level of mine, but not easy either. And he got to know that I had gone through tough times—though not how tough—and had survived sexual abuse. He was my hero. I was his lady. We did ridiculous things together, fell in love, and got married pretty young. It was 1993: he was 21 and I was 22.

Our first marriage to each other had its ups and downs, but we did love each other. We just didn't love God. Nor did we love others in the way that God did. We spent a lot of time privately judging them. We felt we were well qualified to run our own lives and make better decisions than the folks we saw struggling around us. We were definitely not going to duplicate the mistakes of our families. Looking back, our blind arrogance was pretty astounding.

When we had our son in 2000, I found my heart softened

towards God a little. I wasn't as sure that I had made the right choice by shutting Him out; and I wasn't at all sure I should be making a "no God" choice for my son. So I decided to try church again and just see. Will didn't particularly care one way or the other.

We started attending a church and even had Daniel sprinkled as an infant. For a while it was okay. But I found myself calling the pastor one day and tearfully explaining all the doubt and fear and disbelief I struggled with—the truth that I didn't actually know God, though I knew He was real. That I was badly depressed about it. And that I didn't know how to get better.

And the pastor yelled at me. He literally yelled through the phone, asking me what in the world I thought he could do to help me—what I wanted from him. My heart breaks for him today, wondering what crisis of faith I interrupted. But at the time, his reaction confirmed to me that God didn't want me. It was a dead end. And I gave up. We stopped going to church.

For a while, even without God, Will and I muddled along pretty well. But when we hit major life stress (a chronically sick baby, a move back to Arkansas, and a job change all at once), the fact that we were both in the relationship for what we could get out of it, rather than what we could put into it, became a major problem. Will is the one who walked out, but we both did everything that led up to that moment.

During the time we were separated and then finally divorced in 2003, we shared custody of our son and tried very hard to keep his life normal. We also chased after the things we thought were what we needed to make us happy. Will took up Taekwondo, skydiving, and got new drinking buddies. I went back to finish college. My dad, to my amazement, was the one who generously volunteered to make that possible. It was a very loving gesture. I was and am profoundly grateful. But it also did something to me I didn't anticipate when I accepted the gift of money from him: it triggered worse depression because of our history.

By the time I had finished my degree and was looking for a new career, I was in pretty bad shape. My sense that I was "less" and fundamentally unlovable had spiraled out of control. I found myself drinking too much and watching a lot of television. Which is, funnily enough, how I came to Christ—because a pastor named Mark Evans bought commercial airtime to reach lost people like me.

This particular pastor had popped up on my radar several times previously with his "it's not just church, it's life" motto. That evening he told me a baseball story that engaged me enough to want to hear the rest of his message. With friendly and direct simplicity, Mark told me that Jesus loved me no matter what, and that He wanted to change my life forever.

Mark was really different from the pastor who had yelled at me. And I knew Jesus well from the book of Luke. I didn't doubt that Jesus was loving—look at how He forgave the people putting Him to death and gave salvation to the thief crucified next to Him! Truly, there was no one like Jesus. But then…there was God: the Father I didn't understand. That night, after Mark's commercial pep talk, I decided to take a leap of faith and see if God was actually good.

Have you ever let Jesus give you a new life?

My prayer to accept Christ wasn't pretty or eloquent. I wasn't a praying person. (It's funny to think of now.) I just told God that I'd "screwed up my life" and was sorry. I knew my life wasn't headed the direction He had intended, especially my broken marriage. I knew I was powerless to fix it. If He wanted to fix my life, it was His. I wanted what Jesus had to offer. And I offered to do whatever He wanted.

God not only accepted that prayer, He had my ex-husband Will call me the very next day and ask me out on a date. That was an extraordinary act of love to a prodigal daughter. I still marvel at it.

Will had been on his own journey and found himself rethinking the exit from our relationship. We began a new journey together, one that ended with us remarried and eventually becoming members of Mark Evans' church. Will had been baptized as a teen but never followed Jesus before; I was following Jesus and had never been baptized by choice, just sprinkled as an infant. When I got baptized, my dad, of all people—the one who didn't believe in God or Jesus—was the only family member who showed up to watch. He left afterward instead of staying for service, but it meant a lot to me.

So it was then that Will and I really started following Christ. And Pastor Mark Evans had told the truth—Jesus did change our lives forever.

◆◆◆

As I sat at Marriage Night that Friday in May, holding hands with my husband, I also thought about recent changes in our relationship. The previous fall, as we entered the "empty nest" phase, we had gone through a re|engage course on the advice of our Life Groups Pastor, Russ Holmes. Russ had pointed out we could use re|engage as a way to go deeper in our relationship and reconnect around things other than parenting. That was accurate! I highly recommend the re|engage program for marriage transitions, not just marriage problems.

One wonderful thing the course did was clarify our definition of forgiveness. That resulted in my husband stepping up and confessing something to me that he was keeping hidden. His bold trust and my opportunity to extend grace was a blessing to our marriage.

Will's admission was private, not something I'm going to share here. But the lesson re|engage teaches about forgiveness bears repeating, because so many people misunderstand what it is that God is telling them to do.

To paraphrase from Lesson 5 of re|engage: forgiveness is not forgetting (you don't have to pretend nothing happened); it's not reconciling—though it can lead to reconciling (that's a separate process); it's not condoning (if there is something to forgive, something wrong was done); it's not a feeling (you choose to forgive while still hurt, not after you're better); and it's not just about the person who hurt you (holding onto unforgiveness makes you sick). Forgiveness might be instant, or it might be an active process of remembering your commitment to release something to God every single time it hurts again. The bottom line is that you have to acknowledge that God alone has the right to take vengeance. You always need to *"be kind and tender-hearted to one another, forgiving each other just as in Christ God forgave you" (Ephesians 4:32 BSB)*.

That Friday night I tried to believe that maybe forgiveness was available for me, too. My husband was a completely dedicated Christ-follower. But I knew in my heart that my dishonesty was something I should have confessed much earlier—at least at the same time Will made his own bold confession. I couldn't find the inner strength to follow his example...yet.

♦♦♦

That changed Sunday. Our amazing God had already arranged exactly what I needed to gain courage and move forward. He provided the strength I didn't have myself.

Church that day was unusual for me. First of all, instead of being in our large Worship Center like I usually would be, I was in the Community Room at a table with friends watching on a screen. This was significant because it meant I wasn't sitting next to my mom for what was about to happen. God knew that would have been more than I could handle. (It was also better not to be in a crowd that morning. I was in really rough shape and wouldn't have heard a word that was said.)

When I looked at the screen, I saw my friend Will Stevens (now Pastor Will Stevens of vetchurch.org) seated on stage with Pastor Mark. Will proceeded to give a moving testimony about his recent journey to healing. He had been sexually abused at age ten by a scout leader who was employed by a church. I already knew the general outline of Will's story because he had made it public, but this was the first time I had heard his personal testimony. It spoke directly to my wounded soul.

He talked about having been pressured to keep the secret, which he had done; and he talked about what effect that secret burden had placed on him. He said it had made him feel like "damaged goods, guilty, and unworthy" at every phase of his life since he was a child. He talked about building walls to protect himself: how even the ribbons he'd earned in combat from military service were a wall protecting him so that no one would see who he was "underneath all of that". He talked about how, when he had become brave enough to investigate, he had discovered that the man who had abused him had also abused many others across multiple states. That was a lot to come to terms with, but when he did, he found the courage to take action to help others. He held a press conference and told the world what had been done 40 years previously. He said that was the hardest thing he'd ever had to do in his life—harder even than going into active combat.

Will Stevens' story of personal healing was an amazing testimony with the overall lesson that it was absolutely worth it to come forward: he had been given new eyes to see his identity as an heir to the Kingdom of God. God had been with him every step of the way. And to top it off, so had Will's family, his church family, and others in need of his message.

As I sat there trying to absorb how directly God was encouraging me that morning, Pastor Mark launched into a sermon based on Psalm 23, the very Scripture that God had already spoken over me as the basis for what He wanted to do in my life. Mark told me how big God was: that He could handle anything and everything that had ever happened or would happen in my life. Mark pointed out that while my human response to stressful things might be to grasp them tighter and try to fix them myself, that was the path to more stress. In stress-filled times, my security should rest in God's role as my Shepherd, not in myself. God, my Shepherd, would provide rest and relaxation, satisfy my soul, provide detailed direction and protect me. Trusting God—following my Shepherd—was worth doing. And afterwards I should leave a legacy of goodness and mercy.

God could not have made it clearer that my church, The Church at Rock Creek, was a safe place for survivors of sexual abuse to come out of the dark into the light. And after praying that afternoon, I took a baby step. I emailed Mark. I didn't tell him much, just enough for him to know I was struggling with getting help. He responded promptly with gently phrased encouragement. It was the boost I needed to go and do what I really needed to do: talk to my husband. And my sweet husband met me with every bit of grace and compassion that Christ had met him with in his own life. I was no longer alone with my secret. Holding my husband's hand, I stopped resisting and walked into God's valley. I was headed toward real freedom, not the false freedom I'd been running downhill toward years earlier.

PART TWO: THE GOOD SHEPHERD

CHAPTER FOUR: THE PATH

"Trust in the LORD with all your heart, and lean not on your own understanding; in all your ways acknowledge Him, and He will make your paths straight." Proverbs 3: 5-6 BSB

◆◆◆

The first week I started cooperating with God—entered the valley—was a blur of activity. I messaged Will Stevens for some information, told my prayer sisters Shannon and Jan about my history, lined up a therapist appointment for June 10, and saw my doctor for medication. Telling Shannon and Jan about my past—even just as a general outline—was a combination of terrifying and liberating. But I got to see God provide: they both met me like Jesus. Our friendships instantly deepened. Shannon and Jan provided invaluable support.

The next weekend I temporarily deactivated social media. God had prompted me to spend more time physically present with friends and less time online. My obedience led to a major provision. While I was hanging out with my friend Jan, she loaned me Suffering is Never for Nothing by Elizabeth Elliot. It was a great book. On page 52 there was a reference to Joseph's reunion with his brothers in Egypt that caught my attention. So I looked up the verses:

> *"Then Joseph said to his brothers, 'Please come near me.' And they did so. 'I am Joseph, your brother,' he said, 'the one you sold into Egypt! And now, do not be distressed or angry with yourselves that you sold me into this place, because it was to save lives that God sent me before you." (Genesis 45:4-5 BSB)*

It always amazes me how God can use Scripture I've seen many times before and do something new and unexpected with it. In this case, He did two things: for the first time, I connected the suffering inflicted on Joseph with the suffering inflicted on me during my childhood. And the *words "it was to save lives that God sent me before you"* leapt off the page of my Bible...lives, plural.

I had been living with suppressed unanswered "why" questions for years: why would God have allowed my abuse? Why would He have sent me back home when I was 12, rather than rescuing me?

That Scripture started life change. I was now sure of my Heavenly Father's purpose: my childhood suffering wasn't for nothing. While He grieved it because He loved me, He could also see the path that presented the greatest opportunity to minister to others. If I was willing to share my testimony, He could use that to save lives. That rocked my world down to its core. When the dust settled, I had a completely new perspective on the Holiness of God.

But that was still filtered through my inner child's distorted view of the size of the enemy. While I now "got" the purpose of God, she didn't "get" the power of God.

"We were just trying to get Dad saved," she yelled at me, "and now we're headed into a scary valley on a mission to

Do your inner child and adult self have conflict?

'get better and save lives'? Are you kidding me? Why did you tell people? Why did you tell them my secret?"

◆◆◆

God had prepared for that yell years before it happened. He'd done amazing prep work, arranging for me to meet Louise Allison, the founder of PATH (Partners Against Trafficking Humans), fully four years before I'd become desperate for her to speak into my life.

Back in 2015, PATH temporarily owned a building in my neighborhood. They didn't stay: I'm sad to say some neighbors had a fear reaction that the ministry would bring "a bad element" with it. That was heartbreaking.

But while PATH was there, they asked for help with a giant rummage sale to raise money for survivors. And the Spirit led me to go serve. It was almost an out-of-body experience to be involved and still keep my secret hidden.

When I met Louise Allison, I could see Christ in her. She practically glowed. And in the middle of that extraordinarily busy event, she made a point of trying to get to know me—not just once but multiple times. (I think she could see I was hurting, even though I wasn't going to admit it.) Having already seen who Louise was in Christ made me reach out to her when my inner child panicked and yelled. Louise's reply was something I leaned on more than I can say. On the hope that someone who needs help but hasn't asked for it yet might take courage from our interchange, I'm going to share it.

◆◆◆

Louise,

This week I admitted for the first time to my two closest praying partners in Christ and to my husband that my father didn't just sexually abuse me, but that he sold me when I was in elementary school. I was met with compassion and support. I've started some medication and have trauma-based counseling starting

June 10.

At first, I felt like an enormous weight had been lifted off of me, but now that's mixed with a horrible panicky desire to find an undo button and just go back somehow to pretending it never happened, I have no problems, and I've got everything under control. And guilt. Overwhelming guilt that I've talked about this at all.

I just wondered if you could tell me that I've done the right thing and that there's a better future worth all the work I'm about to do. Or even that what I'm feeling is ordinary. Just something.
Carolyn

◆◆◆

Sweet Carolyn,

Thank you so much for sharing this with me. What a brave thing you've done! This is where you leave the world of victim and enter the world of hero.

It is normal to have these mixed emotions and the roller coaster ride will not be easy, but the healing will happen, and the ups and downs will become less each day.

The brave step you've taken is the biggest step towards healing you could make. It says a lot about your character and your trust in the Lord. God will not leave you. Neither will any of those that truly care about you. I will join that group. It would be my honor to walk through this journey with you.

The emotions of guilt, shame and fear, along with other negative emotions, are a deliberate attack from the enemy. Satan does not want you to heal. He wants to keep you broken and lost—trapped in the darkness. I can promise this: you will begin to feel freer, happier, and fuller than you ever have before. Remember that it is very normal for you to experience many different thoughts and emotions. Know that they are coming so that you will not be caught off guard. That's when the enemy tries to attack you the most. Be vigilant, know that it will come, and reach out when it happens—to the Lord and those of us that care about you, knowing that the end result is an unbelievable peace.

When I speak about the abuse, I tell people that I would go through all that pain again to get to the intense joy I have now. This is what is in store for you too. This is the promise of God. The Lord promises that He will never leave you nor forsake you. He promises that if you seek first the kingdom of God that all these things will be added. Trust me when I say that although the road will be rocky and sometimes almost unbearable, the end is worth every bump.

I am so honored that you shared with me and I commit to continual prayer with you and for you. Please let me know if there's anything that you need. As your friend I will be there every step of the way, and as PATH I offer whatever we have, including help to cover the cost of therapy.

For those like you and me who finally come out from behind the darkness and lies, to be around others who share that experience can be soooooo healing so feel free to check out the classes that we offer as well.

Prayer: Lord God, be with Carolyn now and every day as she walks through this healing process. Dispel any lies that try to come against her and show her how well loved she is by You and others. Give her every resource she needs to heal. Surround her with those that will hold her up when she feels weak. I pray Isaiah 61:7 over Carolyn today: "Instead of shame they shall have double honor, And instead of confusion they shall rejoice in their portion. Therefore in their land they shall possess double; Everlasting joy shall be theirs." It's in Your precious Son's name, Jesus Christ, I pray these things. Amen.

Thank you again for sharing! Love, hugs and prayers headed your way.
Louise

♦♦♦

Would it be amazing to change from victim to hero?

If you're being trafficked right now in the United States, call the national hotline for help: 1.888.373.7888 or Text 233733

♦♦♦

If you're a survivor of trafficking (or any type of abuse for that matter) and struggling with the idea of coming forward, please hear me: Louise is telling the truth. It is hard, but absolutely worth it to trust God and get help. Christian counselors, organizations like PATH (pathsaves.org), Celebrate Recovery (celebraterecovery.com) and so many other options are available. God loves you! He wants to heal you. Come into His light.

♦♦♦

I calmed down a lot after Louise's reassurance. But there was still one area I had started panicking about again, and for that, I contacted Pastor Mark Evans.

First, I admitted my history to Mark. Then I confessed that I was still nervously wondering if reality would sink in and my husband would change his mind about staying with me. I asked for help, especially if Will wanted to come in and talk.

Mark immediately said yes to helping us. He also introduced a new concept to me that I had trouble grasping and wasn't sure why. He said, "the PTSD of your pain is an evil that I hope and pray God gives you new ways to deal with".

I had "gotten" that the emotions I was going through were an attack—Louise had been very clear—but for some reason I balked at the truth that the PTSD symptoms could be evil too. I wouldn't understand my discomfort until much later, and when I did, it would be a critical step in my restoration.

I was overwhelmingly grateful for Mark's response, especially his fervent prayer for my healing and courage. I knew I was going to need God's help with both.

Not long after that, I was blessed when my husband fought back against the enemy by writing me a beautiful note about how he would never leave me. I put it in my purse so I could pull it out and be encouraged if the enemy attacked. With that gesture of love, done in Christ's name, Will removed my lingering doubts that our marriage was safe in God's hands.

◆◆◆

I did have one false start in the valley. Rather than trust God to make my path straight, I was going to be "obedient" on my own terms. God had (of course) anticipated that and worked it into His plan.

When I had scheduled counseling, I had known that I wanted a Christian EMDR trauma therapist because of information God had previously put in front of me. And I could see there was one close to home. Unfortunately, she wasn't listed with our insurance. The only similarly skilled therapist listed was in the neighboring town of Benton.

Rather than asking God for direction, I told Him what I

wanted and plunged ahead. I contacted the closer clinic and asked if there was any way that therapist would take my insurance. The answer was no, but that another therapist was coming on board in a few weeks who gladly would—and she had the exact same training.

"Aha!" I thought. "God arranged the new woman just for me!"

It bothered me a little bit that I couldn't check her out in advance. But I shoved that concern to the side.

When I met her on June 10, I found that unlike her counterpart, she wasn't Christian. She believed she had developed a deeper truth by blending things that appealed to her from various cultures and religions. She was a caring person, but that was red flag number one. It didn't seem likely God would send me to her. Red flag number two was that she quoted Jesus—who she didn't believe in—to tell me what the terms of my therapy with her were going to be.

First, she obviously didn't share my goal of speaking Jesus into my dad's life. She gave a little lip service to it, but it wasn't real to her. What was real was to her getting me to be honest about the pain of the past. She talked about Jesus walking in both truth and love in situations, but what she actually quoted to me was how Jesus called out the Scribes and Pharisees as *"whitewashed tombs" (Matthew 23:27 BSB)* and a *"brood of vipers" (Matthew 23:33 BSB)*. She accused me of abusing my inner child's trust every time I met with my dad without doing that, because I wasn't "walking like Jesus". She also insisted that no therapy would work unless I agreed to cut off all contact with my dad for an indeterminate length of time "to get well". Then, she conceded, I could see about speaking Jesus into my dad's life.

I was appalled by the suggestion that I was abusing my inner child. It shook me. I was in no shape to deal with this argument. I wasn't even clearheaded enough to relay the conversation accurately to my pastor, who was more than willing to help me sort it out. I ended up having a pretty dark night of the soul before the fog cleared.

But it did clear. My inner child was certainly mad at my dad about the past, but she was also extremely sad he wasn't saved. Attacking my dad would never win him for Christ. And cutting off all contact with someone who had been going out of his way to make amends for many years was over the top as a boundary reset. What about acting in faith, not fear? *(2 Timothy 1:7)* What about *"I can do all things through Christ who gives me strength"? (Philippians 4:13 BSB)* What about the Great Commission? *(Matthew 28:16-20)*

The end result of my stumble was that God used it to strengthen my faith. I got back up, rejected the therapist's direction, and headed over to see my dad to share the gospel. I hoped to find out, if possible, more about why he didn't want Jesus.

God blessed me with the deepest conversation my dad and I had ever had about faith. I finally learned that he was no longer strictly an atheist.

Would you like your stumbles transformed into strengths?

He admitted that there seemed to be something bigger to the human experience. However, my dad thought some people were created with the capacity for a connection with something greater than themselves, and others were not. His belief, based on his life experience, was that he was pre-wired not to connect with anything greater. So his path was to create the best legacy that he could in the memories of people still living. That was all that would be left after his death. To his eyes, it appeared I was wired for connection, so perhaps my end would be different.

I wasn't sure how to help him, because his beliefs were entrenched. I told him God loved him, but he didn't hear me. I also told him I loved him, wanted him in Heaven with me, and would never stop praying for him. He heard that. He even hugged me and wept. But it didn't seem to change anything. I prayed God would keep working to change his heart.

◆◆◆

The next thing I did was apologize to God for my disobedience about the therapist, ask for direction, and schedule an appointment with that Christian therapist in Benton for June 19. I was starting to "get" that sometimes things "looked wrong" to me because I couldn't see them like God did. I was going to need to start looking at Him instead of circumstance.

To strengthen that concept, He arranged two helpful lessons that summer. The first was an extremely minor car accident on the way to church that took my very old, familiar car away from me and left me driving an unfamiliar modern rental paid for by the other driver's insurance…for almost a month. The minor damage to my car shouldn't have taken a month to get fixed, but it dragged on and on. The end result was that while I did some of the hardest work of therapy in July, I drove home, very tired, in a car that was more comfortable and had many more safety features than the car I would otherwise have been in.

The second lesson was life altering. I had always been someone who didn't just look up directions for a new place I was going but memorized them, turn by turn, and printed out a paper map—and then also ran GPS as backup. Seriously. It meant I was very likely to weigh an invitation to go anywhere unfamiliar against how much energy I had available to do all of that.

The first week I was driving the unfamiliar car back from therapy, there was a problem where power lines went down across the interstate and traffic froze. I had no choice but to change course and rely on my phone's GPS to direct me around...and around...and around the Benton and Bryant area to find a way to get me to Little Rock. At first I was pretty stressed out—I spend all my time in Little Rock where I know the roads—but then the Spirit brought to my mind the verse, *"A man's heart plans his course, but the LORD determines his steps"* (Proverbs 16:9 BSB). I started to laugh. Then I relaxed. By the end of the meandering drive I had become a lot more comfortable with both the rental car and my lack of control over *"my steps"*.

Would you like peace about your direction?

While I do have local area maps downloaded onto my phone in case the internet goes down, I've become a person who types in a destination and takes off, trusting God will get me where I'm going when and if I'm supposed to get there. He taught me Who was in control of my travel arrangements.

That was a practical life lesson in His absolute power over ordinary things. In EMDR therapy I would learn about God's total power over absolutely extraordinary things.

CHAPTER FIVE: FEAR NOT

"Do not fear, for I am with you; do not be afraid,
for I am your God. I will strengthen you;
I will surely help you; I will uphold you with
My right hand of righteousness." Isaiah 41:10 BSB

◆◆◆

A couple of advance words about EMDR therapy, which I found to be a blessing. First, what I'm sharing with you here just skims the surface of intense work that my therapist has done with me. This isn't intended to be any kind of self-help guide. And second, if you have complex trauma, please seek out an EMDR therapist with an EMDRIA certification; don't settle for an EMDR trained clinician. The latter has basic training, but when their knowledge runs out—and it will when treating complex trauma—your therapy is going to get "stuck". That won't be because EMDR doesn't work: it does. There is a directory of therapists available to check out at emdria.org.

◆◆◆

When I entered therapy, God had already repaired much of my sight for who He was. I believed He was a loving Father whom I could trust to provide for me. He had restored my marriage, given me spiritual gifts *(1 Corinthians 12:7)*, a calling *(Ephesians 2:10)*, and made me part of a church family *(Acts 2:42)*. He had also blessed me with a new perspective on the nature of His holiness *(Genesis 45:4-5)*, answering questions about Himself that I'd buried since childhood.

My inner child was still stuck, though. She didn't get the enormity of God's power compared to that of the enemy. Like the blind man in Bethsaida whom Jesus healed in two stages,

I would need more help *(Mark 8:22-26 BSB)*. And God delivered. During therapy, God not only brought His truth into focus but set me free to understand what it meant to be a daughter of the King.

♦♦♦

My new therapist, Rosemary Burns, was both friendly and engaging. Not only was she a Christian, but she also had advanced training credentials the first clinician had lacked. Our initial meeting was mostly history-taking, getting to know each other, and planning what shape my therapy would take.

While I had known that God wanted me in EMDR therapy (because He put it in front of me repeatedly), I hadn't really known why. It was an "aha" moment for me when I learned that just as God created our skin to close after a wound was cleaned out, He had designed our brains to heal naturally when stuck trauma was removed. EMDR worked by removing stuck trauma and letting the brain get better.

We wouldn't start with that right away though: there were exercises my therapist referred to as "resourcing" to do first. And the very first skill she wanted me to learn was something I thought might be a stumbling block for the whole endeavor.

♦♦♦

Never in my memory had I felt physically "safe". But apparently I needed to be able to do exactly that before we did anything else. So I was to imagine a scenario where there were no other people, and I felt good, relaxed, and like "nothing bad could ever happen". Then we'd "install" that safe place to pull up on demand, providing me with relief from the constant tension PTSD placed on my body and mind.

I tried imagining a lot of scenarios—places I had enjoyed being—to see if I could feel "safe" in any of them. Nothing worked during the appointment, so I continued seeking a solution at home.

One place I had high hopes for was a beach in Maui I'd been to years previously. I closed my eyes and remembered the sound and smell of the ocean, the heat of the sun and the warm sand under my feet. But the minute I tried to feel "safe" there, mentally digging my feet into the sand, I instead felt a memory of my dad's hands massaging my feet as a precursor to abuse. I was devastated. Four decades after the fact and I still didn't have mental privacy in my own body.

I sank onto the floor of my bedroom closet, sobbing, and called my dear friend Jamie in Texas. (Like Will, she had been a rock of support when I told her about my history.)

Brokenhearted and scared, I told Jamie I was going to "fail therapy" because I couldn't do the very first exercise. She calmed me down, comforted me, and prayed for God to provide a solution. And God did. He led me to a mental image of my "war room", the area of my house where I often pray, as my "safe place" for the exercise. Focusing on being in His presence would let me feel safe. (I hadn't thought about the fact that "no people" in the scenario didn't have to mean "alone".)

"Installing" the safe place with my therapist was my first experience of bilateral stimulation, a key feature of EMDR. We used "tappers": hand-held devices that vibrated alternately—slowly—against each of my palms while I focused on imagining myself in my "war room" with God. The alternating tapping engaged both sides of my brain and increased its ability to process the work we were doing. (My therapist referred to that as Francine Shapiro's "Adaptive Information Processing" model. Slow tapping is used for installing a resource and can be replicated at home by tapping your hands. Fast tapping is used for processing stored trauma and needs to be monitored by a trained EMDR therapist. If you have PTSD, don't try fast tapping alone at home, especially with one of the tapper kits they sell online. You may trigger a mental health crisis.)

I experienced immediate lowering of my physical and mental stress levels as I "installed" my new safe place. I welcomed the homework to continue practicing multiple times a day. It was an immense blessing just to relax and feel safe in

God's presence.

◆◆◆

Another useful resource my therapist introduced me to was called "container". It was designed to allow me to choose to store difficult memories as they surfaced so that I could work on them with my therapist instead of being overwhelmed by them while I was alone. The imaginary "container" could take any form I wanted, so I pictured an airtight safe I could shove things into and then mentally transfer to a corner of my therapist's office. We "installed" this ability just like we did the safe place.

Would you like some control over difficult memories?

"Container" was hard at first—I wanted to re-open the safe and obsess—but it got easier when paired in prayer with this verse: *"Two are better than one, because they have a good return for their labor. For if one falls down, his companion can lift him up; but pity the one who falls without another to help him up!"* (Ecclesiastes 4:9-10 BSB). God's way didn't come naturally to me, but it was definitely a gentler route to healing.

◆◆◆

A third resource we worked on was called "four elements": a technique to "ground out" from my flashbacks and also from the numbness and disconnect which my therapist labeled as disassociation. She said "four elements" was used after disasters by Humanitarian Assistance Programs (HAP) in their Trauma Recovery Networks (TRN).

We had a visual aid for this exercise: a bracelet with four evenly spaced icons. The bonus was that I could wear the bracelet on difficult days and nights for easy reference.

The first icon on the bracelet was a picture of a mountain (earth). When I looked at it, I was to notice where and how I was sitting or standing and adjust to be more comfortable. I was also to scan my surroundings, take note of three objects and describe them. This would help me to connect to my current physical environment.

The second icon was a picture of swirling wind (air). This was a reminder to pay attention to my breathing. Typically I would stop breathing during a flashback. Instead, I needed to take intentional slow, deep breaths to encourage my body to relax.

The third icon was a water droplet. I learned that part of the fight-or-flight response was to shut off the digestive system, including saliva. That explained why my mouth was always completely dried out during a flashback. By thinking about something like mint or lemon, I could re-moisten my mouth and help break out of that response.

The final icon was the sun (fire). When I looked at the sun, I was to focus on an accomplishment I was proud of: something that made me feel really good. (I focused on the moment my son had graduated from homeschool and headed to college. That was definitely a moment that lit me up.)

Learning the steps to the "four elements" technique was easy. Putting them into practice was hard. For flashbacks, I worked persistently at "grounding out" and started experiencing some control. But for disassociation, even when I started recognizing early symptoms of numbness and disconnect, I wouldn't always try the technique. While the flashbacks were painful and nightmarish, the numbness and disconnect—no longer needed for survival but still a long standing reflex—provided a measure of pain relief that I found difficult to relinquish. It was a problem that God would patiently grow me past.

◆◆◆

The most amazing resource my therapist provided me

with was called "recalibrating affective circuits". She paraphrased Sandra Paulsen's workbook "When There Are No Words" to explain to me that everything I had been through meant my emotions weren't working the way God designed them to anymore. She asked me to think of myself as being like a car where all of the dashboard warning lights had been perpetually on, so I'd clipped the wires to turn off the lights.

Do you ever feel disconnected from your life?

To correct this, we would practice visualizing basic emotions as objects without feeling them. It would be similar to art class, where the teacher might ask you to pick an object to represent a concept. This exercise would allow me to start "seeing" basic emotions so they could become useful sources of information again. We "installed" these concepts, and I gradually started having access to emotional information that had been shut down for years. It's still a novelty to recognize my own anger quickly and be able to deal with it appropriately instead of automatically numbing out and wondering why.

◆◆◆

Once we had these resources in place, and a few more, which took about a month or so of practice, my therapist started guiding me through actual EMDR. The steps to EMDR were straightforward, although each of my individual experiences were pretty different. To make it easier to understand, I've included notes from an example I mentioned in Chapter 2—a time I was drugged by my dad and then trafficked in my childhood bedroom.

- **Pick a strong mental picture from the target event/recurring flashback**
    - I pictured the cup of drugged juice I accepted from my father.
- **Identify a negative self-belief associated with the target event**
    - I'm worthless and trapped.
- **Rate the negative self-belief on the SUD scale ("Subjective Units of Disturbance") (0=no disturbance; 10=greatest disturbance possible)**
    - 10
- **Identify the negative emotion and felt physical symptoms**
    - Despair; stomach pain
- **Identify a positive self-statement I would rather believe**
    - I'm strong and free.
- **Estimate how true that positive self-statement felt on the VOC scale ("Validity of Cognition") (1=Completely False; 7=Completely True)**
    - 2
- **Choose a "safety device" to take along.**
    - I like to take Jesus—He can handle anything.

After we had all of this worked out, I would focus on the mental picture, the negative self-belief, the negative emotion and felt physical symptoms. We would start fast bilateral stimulation. That would trigger processing of the traumatic memory—but rather than "flashing back" into it and just reliving the horrible thing, I would stand outside of it and view it as my adult self.

My therapist would monitor me and let me view the trauma in small doses, interrupting me periodically. My brain would start processing what had been stuck, breaking out of the loop it had been in for years, and the mental picture would shift. (For this particular target, as I stood there holding Jesus' hand and watching events unfold multiple times, I eventually saw my adult self step into the scene, knock the cup of juice out of my dad's hands, tell him off, and rescue my younger self from the house. It was a pretty liberating mental exercise.)

Bit by bit, the traumatic memory we were processing would move down the SUD scale until it hit zero (no disturbance). Once that happened, we would install the chosen positive self-statement until it felt completely true. Then we would test out any known triggers for the flashback and make sure it had been truly defused. Finally, we would envision a future scenario where (Lord forbid) I might have to deal with a similar experience and imagine moving through it to a chosen happy ending.

God showed up faithfully every single time we worked. He set me free from being triggered by different memories, environments, sounds, smells, sights and emotions. It made an enormous difference in my daily life as the flashbacks and nightmares started to diminish. I experienced freedom I had thought was impossible. But with God, nothing *is (Jeremiah 32:27)*.

◆◆◆

I'll never forget one previously "impossible" thing that happened as therapy progressed. I was parked in my car, tired and wistfully thinking about how much I'd like to take a vacation. My mind drifted back to that beach in Maui. I closed my eyes, remembering the ocean waves, the hot sun, and the warm sand. And I realized that I was able to wiggle my bare feet in the sand—no bad memories attached. It was beautiful...just

Would it be helpful to truly relax?

Do you shove down emotions that worry you?

me and God looking out over His creation. He had blessed me with another safe place: my bare feet on His holy ground.

◆◆◆

But I had to wonder: why, after all of this, was I still struggling with one of my original problems—seeing myself as who God said I was? I saw God as more than worthy to assign my value; so what was my problem with accepting who He said I was in Christ? The answer came after a lot of prayer and made me feel both embarrassed and blessed: embarrassed because I hated having to admit to even more irrational problems; and blessed, because it wasn't difficult to tackle with EMDR.

For me, it was simply a matter of language. Words were triggering emotions from trauma and keeping me wrestling with God. I needed to rewrite my core feelings so that my heart—not just my brain—would understand and believe "adopted" and "redeemed" by God when it heard "bought" and "told who I was". Using EMDR, we were able to build a scenario and process those words until there was no pain attached to them. (My ending visual had my inner child all decked out in a princess gown and tiara. She was thrilled. It was just what she needed to understand "child of the King".)

Child of The King

Adopted and Redeemed

◆◆◆

Once I relaxed and started believing I was who God said I

was, I found I suddenly "got" what Mark Evans had said back in the beginning of my valley journey: that the PTSD of my pain was an evil he hoped and prayed God would give me new ways to fight. Seeing myself with open eyes, I was ready to trust God and start fighting the disassociation I had been clinging to as "pain relief". It had been useful for survival years ago, but now it was just something the enemy wanted me shackled to instead of believing I was strong enough, with God's help, to be fully present in uncomfortable situations.

I started praying and really leaning into the verse, *"For God has not given us a spirit of timidity, but of power, love, and self-control" (2 Timothy 1:7 BSB).* And when I found myself reacting to discomfort by numbing out and distancing myself from a situation, I started doing a better job of choosing to "ground" back down.

I trust God to keep working on me in that area—as He has been working on me in so many other areas, both inside and outside of therapy. God has been every bit the Shepherd He promised to be when He brought Psalm 23 to my mind and asked me if I wanted to get well.

CHAPTER SIX: COMFORT

"Even though I walk through the valley of the shadow of death, I will fear no evil, for You are with me; Your rod and Your staff, they comfort me." Psalm 23:4 BSB

◆◆◆

Over and over again, Scripture tells us to "fear not". Easy to say; hard to do. Fortunately, God also promises, *"You will seek Me and find Me when you search for Me with all your heart"* (Jeremiah 29:13 BSB).

I was frequently scared during my trip through the valley and sought God in prayer often. He kept His promise; He was always close. But I found that my adult self was still having a battle with my inner child. The battle was on multiple fronts: whether God could really help me (which she doubted); whether I was really guiltless in what had happened to me (which I doubted); and what in the world to do about forgiveness of men other than my dad (that one was a real tug-of-war).

God chose to take care of the first problem—my inner child's doubt about whether He could really help me—in a surprising (and humorous) way. It both convinced my inner child she could rely on Him and strengthened my adult faith.

◆◆◆

One Saturday morning while I was praying, fairly early in my trip through the valley, God made me aware of an "Under God's Protection" stamp that He'd marked me with. I could sense it hovering over me even I couldn't see it or touch it. It was as if *Ephesians 1:13—"sealed with the promised Holy Spirit"*—became tangible.

I was puzzled and asked God why He was letting me be conscious of this strange phenomenon. But the Spirit said to just say "thank you". So I did. And then I told my husband.

I'd been under intense spiritual attack leading up to that moment. Each day it seemed as if Hell picked out a "Lie Du Jour" to advertise to me, much the same way restaurants push soup to customers. And frankly, I'd been letting the waiter talk me into poor choices.

That Saturday's "lie du jour" was "you're trash"—but I found I could "see" the lie without being tempted to buy it. I wondered if the enemy's selling ability had been limited by what God had done that morning. By evening, I became convinced that was correct.

Does negativity pull you in?

I was in my kitchen making treats to take to Life Group the next morning, and my hands were pretty messy. When I wanted music, I spoke to Siri and told her to play "I Raise A Hallelujah".

Siri was taking her sweet time starting the music, so I looked over at the screen to see what the holdup was. I kid you not, the lockscreen said she was looking for a song called "I Was A Hoe"! Definitely not a song in my library. And SO not what I asked her for.

I stared at the screen in disbelief, mouth agape, and then I started to laugh. Lamest attack by hell ever! It was so ridiculous that I had to share it with Will and my friend Shannon, who laughed too.

Sunday's "Lie Du Jour" was "you don't matter to anyone". Again, I was able to raise an eyebrow and just shrug that one off instead of buying it. Starting early that morning, I got texts and emails from friends who were either thanking me for things I'd done or else needing me to walk alongside them in prayer. It was another particularly lame attack.

Monday's "Lie Du Jour" was "no one wants to hear your story." That was countered immediately by people who knew some of my story contacting me and asking to hear more of my testimony if I was willing to share.

Will and I laughed together. He looked at me and said he thought that God let me be aware of that "Under God's Protection" stamp because He wanted me to watch Him make short work of the enemy—to watch move and countermove. That was both amazing and incredibly funny to me.

So much of my childhood, the enemy loomed over me like he filled the universe. After that weekend, my inner child saw the truth: God doesn't just fill the universe—He created it. He *"stretches out the heavens and treads on the waves of the sea" (Job 9:8 BSB)*. Abba was someone who could—and would—provide good help when needed.

Do you know God can and will help you?

After I learned that lesson, the tangible sense of a hovering stamp of protection faded away. But I'll never forget it. And I know I'm sealed permanently by the One Who saved me.

❖❖❖

The second battle God took on was getting me to stop beating up on myself for my past. I couldn't shake irrational feelings of guilt that I somehow should have been able to stop everything that had happened. It was part of why so many of the attacks of the enemy were effective.

Are you carrying guilt that isn't yours to carry?

What I didn't realize was that all that anger I was feeling at myself…was directed at my inner child. I was basically beating up on her. God knew that, though. And like any good parent, He stepped in to correct me.

◆◆◆

The previous year my mom had passed a lot of family pictures on to me. I had thought I would sort them out at some point but hadn't done it yet. The Spirit started to get very insistent about getting that box of photos out of the cabinet. I resisted for a while, but ultimately went and started to go through them. I found that I was being directed to look specifically for pictures of myself from second to fifth grade. And despite the large volume of old photos, I found those pictures pretty easily.

I lined them up on the carpet and looked at little me. I had the strange realization that I was looking at my inner child.

As I looked at each image in turn, I caught my breath. With multiple years of pictures lined up in order, I could literally watch the light go out of my eyes. I could see how progressively unwell I looked. I could see the sadness and the pain.

And I could see how small I was.

My heart broke for my inner child. I would never expect this tiny person to be able to "handle things and get them under control"—words I kept throwing at myself over my past. It wasn't just unreasonable; it was outrageous.

And then it got worse. I saw another picture, one from little me's birthday party. And in that picture, I was having to kiss a man "thank you" for the birthday present he had given me.

I stared in shock. I recognized him. He was one of the men my dad let abuse me. And there he was, at my childhood party. Collecting a kiss. I couldn't wrap my head around what I was seeing.

I had forgotten so much about being little me. But I began to remember.

I remembered what it was like to recover from being drugged, and how sick I felt. I remembered what it was like to be in situations so unbearable that I floated out of my body and observed myself from a distance. I remembered what it was like to have physical injuries that got hidden and neglected. I remembered the nights I slept huddled in my closet downstairs, hoping it would somehow hide me and protect me.

I remembered the loneliness. I remembered the shame. I remembered the anger. And I remembered the despair. Despair is a terrible thing at any age. At 8, it led me to actions that were both sad and poignantly funny.

◆◆◆

My spirit was deeply wounded after I was trafficked at home in my own bedroom. Drugged, used, and discarded—not even re-dressed. Left naked, dirty, and under a sheet. No place was safe anymore. I wanted out, and for the first time it occurred to me that death could provide that.

I knew very little about death. But I did know that my mom warned me not to be outside in winter without my coat or that would be the end result. I had no reason to disbelieve her: no coat in winter equaled freezing to death.

I thought hard and came up with a plan.

When it got cold outside—cold enough that all the kids were in winter coats, noses streaming, breath visible as they ran around the school playground—I ran and hid when the playground aide blew the whistle to line up and go back inside.

We had three "wells" on our playground: giant, roof-covered tractor tires painted in bright primary colors. I climbed into the yellow "well" and waited for the playground to clear. Eventually, the familiar clamor of kids faded away. I was left alone listening to random traffic sounds, wind in the trees, and my own rapidly pounding heartbeat.

I sat up inside the "well" and took off my coat. I struggled for a minute—I was clumsy with nervousness, and had trouble getting out of the mittens my mom had strung through my coat sleeves.

Freed, I pressed myself up against the inside of the tire, thinking it would be cold enough to speed up the process. It made my teeth chatter, but nothing else happened. After a few minutes, I started considering moving to another piece of playground equipment: the large metal pipes we crawled through and sat in. I thought for sure they'd be much colder.

I poked my head up out of the "well", saw I was alone, and made a beeline for the pipes. I climbed in and pressed myself out full-length. I even took off my shoes and socks. Again, it made my teeth chatter, but nothing else happened. I started to cry.

At that point, I became aware of something with me. It encouraged me to dry my tears, put on my socks and shoes, get my coat, enter the building through a particular door and go sit down in my classroom like nothing had happened. It assured me I wouldn't get in trouble. Today I wonder if it was an angel. I had no idea then. But I took the advice and was able to slip back into the school routine without being caught and punished.

◆◆◆

There is some sad humor in remembering that day. There isn't any in remembering the continuing despair. I remember going through bathroom cabinets as I got older, looking for the means to end my life—debating endlessly, teetering on the brink of a permanent decision multiple times. It was only through the grace of God Himself that I made it through childhood and into adulthood. I believe He protected me from myself more times than I remember.

◆◆◆

Sitting on the carpet, looking at the photos lined up in front of me, I apologized profusely to my inner child. I told her how proud I was of her for surviving unbelievably awful situations. I promised never again to blame "little me" for anything outside of her control—ever. And then I thanked God for arranging for me to have pictures I would otherwise never have had and correcting my lifelong view of the entire situation. That left just one more large, ongoing battle between me and my inner child: how in the world to forgive men like the one in the picture from my birthday party.

◆◆◆

Forgiving my dad was one thing. He'd been working for years to be a better father. Forgiving the other people...that was a big question mark.

There were two problems. My inner child wanted to "forgive" them, so they'd just go away—she was angry and afraid. She didn't want to deal with it or think about them. Adult me was just so angry, especially in light of what I was remembering, that I wanted to beat the crud out of something or someone—not forgive anyone.

"Forgiving" in name only out of fear wasn't an option; failing to forgive wasn't an option either. I thought about the parable of "The Unforgiving Servant" and contemplated what to do.

◆◆◆

"Then Peter came to Jesus and asked, 'Lord, how many times shall I forgive my brother who sins against me? Up to seven times?'

Jesus answered, 'I tell you, not just seven times, but seventy-seven times!

Because of this, the kingdom of heaven is like a king who wanted to settle accounts with his servants. As he began the settlements, a debtor was brought to him owing ten thousand talents. Since the man was unable to pay, the master ordered that he be sold to pay his debt, along with his wife and children and everything he owned.

Then the servant fell on his knees before him. 'Have patience with me,' he begged, 'and I will pay back everything.'

His master had compassion on him, forgave his debt, and released him.

But when that servant went out, he found one of his fellow servants who owed him a hundred denarii. He grabbed him and began to choke him, saying, 'Pay back what you owe me.'

So his fellow servant fell down and begged him, 'Have patience with me, and I will pay you back.'

But he refused. Instead, he went and had the man thrown into prison until he could pay his debt.

When his fellow servants saw what had happened, they were greatly distressed, and they went and recounted all of this to their master.

Then the master summoned him and declared, 'You wicked servant! I forgave all your debt because you begged me. Shouldn't you have had mercy on your fellow servant, just as I had on you?' In anger his master turned him over to the jailers to be tortured, until he should repay all that he owed.

That is how My heavenly Father will treat each of you unless you forgive your brother from your heart." (Romans 12:14-21 BSB)

◆◆◆

My inner child pointed out that "fear of the Lord" was reasonable.

I pointed out that God wanted me to "forgive from [my] heart"—really forgive, not just say some words and block it out.

She sulked.

I beat up our living room ottoman to let off some steam.

This went on for a while. Some days were pretty dark.

One night, it finally was too much. I was on my bed, my husband beside me, talking it through out loud with both

Have you ever struggled with forgiveness?

him and God. I couldn't stand the tension anymore. It was physically, emotionally and spiritually crippling me.

I turned my inner focus to an image of Jesus on the cross. I thought about everything that I knew from Scripture that led to that moment. I pictured it in graphic detail. I looked at Him.

And I loved Him. I knew I loved Him before that moment, but my heart became so full of worship for Him that I would gladly have given Him anything that He wanted.

And that was the key.

"Jesus," I told my husband, "wants me to forgive the men. And Jesus deserves whatever He wants. It's not really even about the men—it's about Jesus."

I let gratitude and worship flood the dark places in my heart, envisioning Jesus on that cross. And in the presence of my husband, I asked God for forgiveness for my unforgiveness, and then I forgave, out loud and from my heart, the men who had treated me so badly. Not because they deserved it, but because Jesus did.

It took every ounce of strength in my body. I was literally limp and unable to move for quite a while afterwards. I cried a lot. But afterwards I started to feel better. And the hold the men had on me was lost—my inner child actually got what she wanted when I did what God wanted done the way He wanted it done.

God's comfort wasn't worldly. God's comfort was holy. And it was an important step in my journey to healing and happiness.

PART THREE:
I SHALL NOT WANT

CHAPTER SEVEN: THE TABLE PREPARED

"You prepare a table before me in the presence of my enemies."
Psalm 23:5a BSB

◆◆◆

About the same time that I started therapy, Pastor Greg Kirksey preached another sermon that I found helpful. It was part two of a series entitled "Only God Knows: Experiencing Hope While Living With Life's Unanswered Questions".

This was shortly after I had gotten the answer to my own unanswered question of why. The Spirit had led me to the story of Joseph, specifically to the verse, *"do not be distressed or angry with yourselves that you sold me into this place, because it was to save lives that God sent me before you" (Genesis 45:5 BSB)*. I was already sure that God had a higher purpose for my pain and suffering.

But PTSD had my focus scattered. And my past had my identity shattered. I needed more than "why". "Why" didn't address all the feelings that I was having.

Greg preached that day about the "difference in a head knowledge and a heart knowledge". He encouraged us to grow our faith by taking control of our focus. And then something happened I'll never forget.

In the middle of listing all sorts of different circumstances that people go through, Greg turned my direction and said, "You may have been abused—horribly abused, unspeakably abused; it's awful."

Greg then shifted back toward the front and continued. "But that is not your identity. Hardship is not your identity. Your hardship does not define you—God does! Meditate on who you are: I am IN Christ! Meditate on that. When you take on the label of victim and restrict your view of yourself to that experience, you trouble your trouble. You restrict your hope.

Your power and potential become limited. Christ IN you—the hope of glory. Meditate on the fact that Christ is in you."

I was left shaking in my seat by having the line about abuse spoken in my direction. (He knew nothing about my history at this point. He obviously does now.)

Later I pulled up the stored online stream of the earlier service just to see if Greg had made the same remark to them. He had not. He had only said those words in the service that I attended.

The delivery of those words was perfectly timed to get my attention. I believed God wanted me to understand that help for my heart would come from knowledge of who I was in Christ.

At the end of that sermon, I took the three action points Greg taught us and wrote my own note. It simply said:

MEDITATE
Christ is *IN* you.
Christ is *WITH* you.
Christ is *FOR* you.

I put one copy on my mirror and one on my prayer wall. Despite all the turmoil PTSD was causing me, this was something I could do. And I did. I started intentionally pausing and focusing. That laid important groundwork, because God didn't just want to mend my heart with those truths: He wanted to equip me for battle.

◆◆◆

The enemy certainly isn't on the level of God, but it would be foolish to underestimate him. He is well aware of humanity's greatest weak points—and of my own particular areas of sin. When I was at my most vulnerable, he struck.

For the first time in many years, as I suffered flashbacks to the darkest period of my life, the temptation to self-harm began to dangle in front of me. I was flabbergasted, horrified, and unsure what in the world to do.

Self-harm and suicidal thinking are not the same. To an outside eye it might appear to be related, but the motivation is different. Self-harm is about gaining control of pain, not ending your life. In a twisted sort of way, it's about pain relief.

I understood why the temptation had re-entered my life: everything felt out of control and everything hurt. But I also remembered very well that hurting myself was a dead end road that led to spiritual pain, guilt, and the desire to run and hide from God.

Years ago, my life had simply improved enough that the temptation to self-harm had gone away. This time, I realized I was going to have to fight. The question was, how?

I looked up suggestions online and wasn't impressed. Every one of them seemed to be about substituting something that would continue to feed my emotional addiction while preserving my physical body. Drawing lines on myself with red ink, freezing myself with ice cubes, snapping a rubber band into my skin—every suggestion I read ignored the reality that my soul was what was really in trouble.

Blessedly, I had the Word in my heart. The Spirit was able to bring verses to my mind to help me.

The first was *"[n]o temptation has seized you except what is common to man. And God is faithful; He will not let you be tempted beyond what you can bear. But when you are tempted, He will also provide an escape, so that you can stand up under it"* (1 Corinthians 10:13 BSB). This was a promise I could stand on: with God, there was a way out.

Next came *"[t]wo are better than one, because they have a good return for their labor. For if one falls down, his companion can lift him up; but pity the one who falls without another to help him up!"* (Ecclesiastes 4:9-10 BSB). And then *"[t]herefore confess your sins to each other and pray for each other so that you may be healed. The prayer of a righteous man has great power to prevail"* (James 5:16 BSB). From these verses, it was clear that God's plan for me was to fight with help, and to fight in prayer.

Finally, the Spirit brought to my mind, *"[t]hese words I am commanding you today are to be upon your hearts...Tie them as reminders on your hands and bind them on your foreheads. Write them on the doorposts of your houses and on your gates" (Deuteronomy 6:6,8 BSB).* These verses took my breath away, because I realized what God was telling me to do; and for me, it was going to take even more humility than asking for prayer. It would take a true act of surrender.

I was going to have to write Scripture references directly on my skin. I needed a wall of Truth in between me and temptation.

Two of the areas I needed to write on were going to be places people might notice. I hated that idea. But there was no way around it: God was clear that for me, this was the path He was making available.

I cried for a while. Then I prayed and set out to learn what verses God had in mind that would help me love *Him "with all [my] heart and with all [my] soul and with all [my] strength" (Deuteronomy 6:5).* And that was when He took the meditation truths to the next level.

❖❖❖

There were three verses I needed in my heart and on my flesh:
- *"Do you not know that your body is a temple of the Holy Spirit who is in you, whom you have received from God?" (1 Corinthians 6:19a BSB)*
- *"For God has not given us a spirit of timidity, but of power, love, and self-control." (2 Timothy 1:7 BSB)*
- *"I can do all things through Christ who gives me strength." (Philippians 4:13 BSB)*

The first verse reminded me that I wasn't alone in my flesh. Christ was in me. That definitely gave me pause. The second verse was a positive confession of all the power that came with that togetherness. Christ was with me. The third verse affirmed that power was there for me to use. Christ was for me.

I wrote the first two verse references on my palms. I

couldn't avoid seeing them. When temptation loomed, I could have a literal "talk to the hand" moment with the enemy, reciting the verses aloud.

The third verse I used as the final barrier protecting the flesh I was tempted to damage.

After this step of obedience, I took a giant leap of faith and went to my friends Shannon and Jan. I confessed my struggle, showed them the Scripture references on my palms, and asked them to lay hands on me and pray. They were startled, and it showed; but they were more than willing to fight alongside me.

I also confessed to my husband and asked him for his help. He held me in a giant bear hug while he prayed. He was well aware of what I had gone through previously and was proud of me for fighting back.

It was extraordinarily humbling and not a little bit scary to be that vulnerable. But it also started making the burden lighter.

I had to write and rewrite those verse references on my skin over time as they washed away. And even with all that help, I still slipped once.

It was on a night I was foolish enough to have a drink. Alcohol and my depression was a terrible combination. The slip left me devastated and wishing I could roll back time by even a few minutes. I obviously couldn't.

It was then that the Spirit brought to my mind a fourth verse: *"Therefore, there is now no condemnation for those who are in Christ Jesus. For in Christ Jesus the law of the Spirit of life has set you free from the law of sin and death" (Romans 8:1-2 BSB).*

My identity in Christ meant that I could confess, repent, and be fully restored. I could get back up.

After I did that, I also went

Do you know God never stops loving you?

to my husband, told him the truth, and was met with grace and encouragement—not judgement. It was a powerful moment for me.

My temptation toward self-harm went away as the EMDR therapy progressed. I don't have to write those verse references on myself anymore. But I'm fully equipped to fight on solid ground if the enemy ever attacks me there again.

◆◆◆

It's important to share that Will and I had one more bad experience with alcohol. We discovered that it combined just as badly with an anger-filled flashback as it did with my urge to self-harm. I'm embarrassed to admit that after a few drinks and in the midst of a flashback, I didn't just beat up our mattress—no piece of furniture was safe from me during that time period—I also yelled at my sweet husband like he was my enemy. That was the end of all social drinking for me. My temple and our marriage were both too valuable. If you're struggling with past trauma and have more than a social drinking habit—in other words, if just stopping isn't an option for you—I encourage you with all my heart to check out Celebrate Recovery. Your temple and marriage are worth it too.

◆◆◆

Back at the end of 2018 when Greg had preached about Christ-centered happiness, starting me on my journey, he emphasized several things—all of which needed my attention. I couldn't truly keep my distance from the world, delight in the Word, or be devoted to the work of God while I was finding my identity in shifting sand. I needed healing.

Today, I fully see myself as a child of God *(John 1:12)*. And I have experienced the truth of Him setting a table for me in the presence of my enemies *(Psalm 23:5a)*.

I still meditate on "Christ is in me, Christ is with me, and Christ is for me". But I also meditate on this: *"Finally, brothers, whatever is true, whatever is honorable, whatever is right, whatever is pure, whatever is lovely, whatever is admirable—if anything is excellent or praiseworthy—think on these things"* (Philippians 4:8 BSB).

In my daily life, when someone throws the word "whatever" at me, it's usually accompanied by an eye roll. That's not the usage here. This "whatever" is the Greek word "hosos", which according to Thayer's Greek Lexicon means "as much as", "as great as", or "as long as". In other words, this "whatever" is about thinking BIG. This verse is an invitation to dream in the presence of God Himself.

As I tentatively started dreaming of what God could do with my testimony—my fish and loaves, as it were—He started arranging what I can only call divine appointments with other women. These were also survivors of sexual trauma, most of whom began their stories with "I can't believe I'm telling you this—I haven't even told my own husband." The burdens they were carrying were heavy.

It's amazing to think back to how convinced I was that people would run from me in horror if they knew my story. I suppose someone still might. But so far women have sat across a table from me, hope lighting up their eyes, as they take their own leap of faith and share their pain for the first time. And it's hearing my own story that frees them from worry that I'll judge them for theirs. Who would have thought that my history could become that kind of blessing? (God, apparently. Because He can do WHATEVER.)

I love these women. Some of them have become good friends; others have been people I met in passing to share a meal or coffee with one time. But I love all of them. And I pray for each of them.

Last year, I was scared to death to talk about my past. Now I routinely do and get to tell people God wants to heal them. In this broken world, that definitely qualifies as God setting the table.

◆◆◆

If I was sitting across from you in a coffeeshop or restaurant, and you were telling me your story—first of all, I would be honored. But if you started it with "I've never told my husband", I would want you to know just how big of a weapon that is in the hands of the enemy. The devil can use it to cause unbelievable confusion and heartache in a marriage. He did in mine.

I am a big believer in both individual Christian counseling and Christian marriage counseling. And not just for the obvious reason—defeating the thief's desire *"to steal and kill and destroy" (John 10:10a)*. But also because of what I'm going to talk about next: how "whatever is lovely" in marriage includes spiritual intimacy, both in the bedroom and in daily life. Trusting God with my journey and getting help led to amazing changes I never anticipated.

CHAPTER EIGHT: OVERFLOW

"You anoint my head with oil; my cup overflows."
Psalm 23:5b BSB

◆◆◆

The point of marriage isn't to "live happily ever after" in some blissed-out state like the ending of a fairy tale. (No one does that anyway.)

It's also not just to have companionship, help paying the bills, or even to have kids. Those are good things, but they're not the ultimate goal.

God designed marriage for us to grow towards Christ-likeness together (Ephesians 5:22-33). The ultimate goal is pursuing a holy happiness which shines God's light in this broken world.

Do you want God's best for your marriage?

When Will and I were focused on what we could get out of marriage rather than what we could put into it, we were very vulnerable to daily life stress. As trouble piled on, derailing what we wanted for ourselves, we grew dissatisfied. We started picking at each other over unmet, unvoiced and sometimes even unrecognized expectations. We fought. We grew distant. And then finally, we divorced.

When we got remarried, we were both committed to following Jesus. We started shifting our pattern towards what we could do for one another rather than what we could get from one another *(Philippians 2:1-8)*.

That took a long time to learn, and it didn't come naturally.

We participated in many years of couples Bible studies as we walked and grew together.

When we finally surrendered our remaining strongholds to God, trusting Him enough to trust each other fully, God improved our marriage dramatically *(Matthew 6:33)*. A level of peace grew between us that had never existed. And out of that peace grew the freedom to play, to dream and to pursue life together in a different way. Putting what God wanted first changed everything.

◆◆◆

I told you in an earlier chapter that Will had admitted something to me that I didn't know, giving me the opportunity to extend grace where he felt he needed it. Afterwards he relaxed with me. He was just different! Being seen and loved where he had been harboring doubts about how I'd react denied the devil room to whisper into our marriage *(James 4:7)*. And when I trusted God and told Will the truth about my childhood, that effect intensified. I was able to relax with him too.

Because we already shared the common goal of following Christ, honesty enhanced our marriage; it didn't destroy it. Hundreds of little things over the years where we had misunderstood each other were suddenly explained. We could communicate completely freely for the first time. The way we joked with each other changed; the level of sharing we did about our personal struggles changed; our openness for stepping out together in faith changed. And not surprisingly, our sex life changed.

I say not surprisingly, but actually, to me, it was a surprise. I couldn't really figure out what was going on. It wasn't that we were doing anything particularly different, it was just definitely much better.

I was puzzled enough that I found myself bringing it up in therapy. And my therapist asked me a question I honestly didn't "get" at first. She asked, "When you've been with your husband before, have you been with *him*?"

I pretty much just looked at her in confusion. So she repeated herself. "Have you been with him?"

I wanted to say well, of course, what in the world do you mean. But then it clicked.

I started to think about it and realized that up until that point, the answer was usually "no". Sex was something fun I did with Will, but it wasn't a spiritual event. I wasn't particularly thinking about him as a person.

My therapist said that depersonalizing sex is pretty common for survivors of sexual abuse. It starts as a survival mechanism that provides a mental "exit" from unbearable events. But it sticks around as a mental change long after the trauma is over. Since it had been lifelong for me, I didn't know enough to notice.

As I got better, I didn't need to depersonalize sex. When I was with Will, I was able to pay attention to him, the man I loved, and my responses reflected that. His responses changed as my responses changed. And the type of connection we had went from purely physical to something much more profound.

◆◆◆

As I've talked to other survivors of sexual abuse, I've found that some avoid sex altogether; some alternate between avoiding sex and using substances to numb out and have sex; some depersonalize and view sex as physical recreation; and some have gone through pornography and sex addiction. There's not a single response to trauma—and there are probably responses I have yet to encounter. But untreated trauma from sexual abuse can definitely rob survivors and their spouses of the joy in intimacy that God intended for marriage (Song of Solomon:1-8). And that's heartbreaking. My prayer is that my own transparency might help at least one other survivor choose to step forward on a journey toward something better.

◆◆◆

Another change that surprised me, but in retrospect probably shouldn't have, was how much Will's leadership in our household started growing. He had already begun shepherding me more when he felt fully accepted. But when I stopped hiding my struggles and let him really get to know me, he quickly went from being a very good husband to a truly great one.

He invested time—an amazing amount—in learning about trauma and PTSD. He asked questions; he listened (to hear, not just to respond); and he even did external reading.

He learned how grounding worked so he could prompt me to help myself during flashbacks. He made time to be present and just hold me when there was nothing he could possibly say to make things better. He reminded me to be patient with myself when the road seemed incredibly long. And he literally prompted me to eat and get more sleep when things were particularly hard.

It was through Will's massive outpouring of love that I learned something I never knew about myself. Years before, when we had worked through The 5 Love Languages® by Dr. Gary Chapman, I had determined that my primary love language was words of affirmation. But I was wrong. My primary love language was actually quality time.

Living behind walls in my life with Will meant that not only had I not been fully with *him* in the bedroom, I hadn't been fully *with* him in general. Ironically, the very thing I was doing to protect myself was hurting me. God knew that. And so as I healed He blessed me by prompting Will to lavish me with exactly the type of love I was designed to delight in.

Having my need for quality time met changed other things. The more loved I felt by Will, the more I looked to him in ways I never had. I found myself going to him and telling him my prayer needs so he could pray over me, not just pray for me during his daily prayer time when he was alone. I found myself talking to him about things going on in my life looking for actual solutions, not just for a listening ear. I also found myself spending more time thinking about what he might want or appreciate than I ever had before and making choices that reflected that.

Basically, the more loved I felt, the more respect I showed. And if you've ever read *Love & Respect* by Dr. Emerson Eggerichs (another marriage study we truly enjoyed), you'll know that's a pattern of behavior that creates a positive loop. The more respect I showed, the more love Will expressed. The end result was that both of us, even in the middle of a really hard walk, started having more fun with each other than we normally did. We began actively looked for opportunities to play together. And that culminated in a skydiving trip.

◆◆◆

Back when we were separated and then divorced, one of the things Will started doing was skydiving. First he did a tandem jump, where he was tethered to a licensed instructor; and then he started doing solo jumps.

Will loved the thrill of freefall and the peacefulness of riding the chute down afterwards. He talked it up for a long time, but I wasn't ever tempted. The hyperawareness problems I spent a lifetime trying to conceal were wearying; I had no interest in activities that would add to my adrenaline levels.

As I got better, that changed. EMDR helped so that I wasn't hyperalert and worn out all the time. When I stopped dealing with daily adrenaline overload, I found myself enjoying activities that I never would have previously. And I started wondering about skydiving.

On Sunday, January 19, 2020, I took the plunge. Will and I drove up from Little Rock to a great facility, Skydive Fayetteville, so I could do my first tandem jump. To say I was excited would be an understatement.

The paperwork and video warnings they made me go through were dire—I joked with Will that they reminded me of things I had to sign before having surgery. And during the pre-jump training session I was taken aback to realize that if something happened to the instructor on the way down, he was relying on me to do the right things and save both of us! The reality that his life was in my hands too had never occurred to me. He stepped me through what to do; and I sent up a special prayer request to God to have that covered.

It was close quarters in the little plane. There was a really nice 18 year old (Adam, who was doing a tandem jump to celebrate his birthday), me, two instructors, and our pilot. All of us jumpers were buckled to the floor, tightly squeezed together. (That was an icebreaker in and of itself. There was a lot of joking.)

The plane ride, swiftly ascending to 10,000 feet, was more exciting than I had anticipated. I found myself wanting to learn to fly the little plane. (When I told my husband later, he said he'd like to also. Now it's on our bucket list of things to do together.)

Having the plane door get opened at 10,000 feet was an experience. There was an intense rush of cold air, sound, and for a first time jumper like me, a sense that I might get sucked out. (The instructors had warned us just before opening the door and said to stay calm. So I mostly did.)

Adam got to jump first. He and his instructor crawled into position together; and then off they went.

My instructor signaled me to get into the prearranged spot. We both kneeled on our left knees and put our right feet out on the step. The view was incredible. So was the wind.

We rocked back and forth—1, 2, 3—and then we let go and fell forward together out of the plane. After we cleared it, my instructor signaled me. We threw our arms out, looked up at the horizon, and freefell for about 5,000 feet. It was every bit as amazing as Will had said.

At Skydive Fayetteville, tandem jumpers get to pop the chute and take a turn steering around (which was pretty simple—pull right and you go right; pull left and you go left). While I steered, my instructor acted as a tour guide, pointing out all the interesting things we could see from our aerial view. Then he took control of the chute. After we practiced the move we would do when we came in for a landing, we headed for the field.

I looked for my husband on the ground as we soared in, and there he was. He was too small for me to see that he was filming me with his phone. But I knew in my heart he was grinning, because he had been as I went up in the plane. And his smile lights up my world.

The approach was smooth and simple. My instructor was really good. All I had to do was tuck my legs up and trust things would go well. Then we were on the ground. And I found myself smiling so big my cheeks hurt for a while.

My friend Shannon has told me that skydiving isn't for her. (Multiple times. Like I'm going to seize her and throw her out of a plane! Not.) And I totally get that. But it was important for me. The experience proved to be way more than just an adrenaline rush.

Have you ever taken a leap of faith?

For me, I found a peace in the freefall, not just in floating down under the parachute. There was something liberating about being totally committed to a course of action.

Skydiving was a leap of faith where I trusted that God was really in control. And for the rest of my life when I face something challenging, I know that I'm someone who, with God, can jump out of an airplane. (My equivalent of *Psalm 18:29*.) In fact, it's something I plan to do again.

❖❖❖

The skydiving trip was amazing. I was so glad that my husband encouraged me to step out of my comfort zone and go for it!

But he's done much more than cheer me on from the sidelines as I've started taking leaps of faith for God. He has prayed for me, listened at length, encouraged me, and brought wisdom from his own studies and reading into the equation. I have truly been blessed beyond measure by what God has done with our marriage.

CHAPTER NINE:
GOODNESS AND MERCY

"Surely goodness and mercy will follow me all the days of my life, and I will dwell in the house of the LORD forever."
Psalm 23:6 BSB

◆◆◆

There are two Bible stories that I thought about a lot as God healed me. The first one was from the New Testament. The second was from the Old Testament. The first story was about a healing that Jesus performed, and how the recipients reacted.

The Ten Lepers
"While Jesus was on His way to Jerusalem, He was passing between Samaria and Galilee. As He entered one of the villages, He was met by ten lepers. They stood at a distance and raised their voices, shouting, 'Jesus, Master, have mercy on us!'

When Jesus saw them, He said, 'Go, show yourselves to the priests. And as they were on their way, they were cleansed.

When one of them saw that he was healed, he came back, praising God in a loud voice. He fell facedown at Jesus' feet in thanksgiving to Him—and he was a Samaritan.

'Were not all ten cleansed?' Jesus asked. 'Where then are the other nine? Was no one found except this foreigner to return and give glory to God?

Then Jesus said to him, 'Rise and go; your faith has made you well!'" (Luke 17:11-19 BSB).'

Lepers were untouchables, separated from living ordinary life within the community. I wondered why in the world only one of the men came back to say thank you after experiencing something so restorative. My husband reminded me that the rules said you had to present yourself to the priest before you could be accepted by others *(Leviticus 14)*—and the Jews were often more preoccupied with rules and community acceptance than with giving glory to God. The Samaritan lived differently.

I found I had a deeper understanding of that as I received my own healing. I discovered that a longing for "normalcy" in community can easily become a false idol. But when God heals us, it is for His glory, not our own. As Scripture says, *"[b]lessed be the God and Father of our Lord Jesus Christ, the Father of compassion and the God of all comfort, who comforts us in all our troubles, so that we can comfort those in any trouble with the comfort we ourselves have received from God. For just as the sufferings of Christ overflow to us, so also through Christ our comfort overflows"* (2 Corinthians 1:3-5 BSB).

To fail to respond to God's healing with gratitude and worship would be lukewarm faith at best. And that's not a faith I want *(Revelation 3:16)*.

The second story I thought about a lot was the story of Shadrach, Meshach and Abednego *(Daniel 3)*. In that Scripture, King Nebuchadnezzar set up a giant golden statue of himself and commanded everyone to worship it. But Shadrach, Meshach and Abednego refused. They remained loyal to God.

King Nebuchadnezzar confronted them and threatened to throw them into a fiery furnace if they didn't comply and worship his statue. He also asked what god would save them from his punishment.

The three men replied: *"'King Nebuchadnezzar, we do not need to defend ourselves before you in this matter. If we are thrown into the blazing furnace, the God we serve is able to deliver us from it, and he will deliver us from Your Majesty's hand. But even if he does not, we want you to know, Your Majesty, that we will not serve your gods or worship the image of gold you have set up'"* (Daniel 3:16-18 NIV).

Even if God didn't save them from the blazing fiery furnace, they would still worship only Him. Their obedience wasn't dependent on circumstances. Their obedience demonstrated unconditional love *(John 14:21)*.

God did choose to save Shadrach, Meshach and Abednego. He didn't let them face the furnace alone. *"[T]he fire had no effect on the bodies of these men. Not a hair of their heads was singed, their robes were unaffected, and there was no smell of fire on them"* (Daniel 3:27). It amazed King Nebuchadnezzar so much that he decreed a death sentence on anyone who offended their God *(Daniel 3:28-29)*.

The miracle was astounding. But it was the "even if" faith that really captured my attention. I didn't know if I had that kind of faith in me.

And then God put it on my heart to write this book.

◆◆◆

At first, I couldn't fathom writing my story down. It was one thing to tell a few people what I'd been through or to meet with other survivors: writing would be a completely different level of sharing. It was terrifying to think of complete strangers reading my story in my absence.

As God drew me along His path, the enemy attacked by suggesting that all the pain involved in writing would be for nothing. He suggested that no one would even bother to read my story—that not one person would be helped. He also suggested that lots of people would read my story and that the reaction would be devastatingly negative. (The devil's attacks are often diametrically opposed in content because he's the *"father of lies" [John 8:44 BSB]).*

The Spirit helped me recognize that EVEN IF that happened—no one read the book, or everyone did and my life blew up—my obedience was valuable. My job was to give God my loaves and fish. Whatever followed—hosos—was up to God, not me *(Luke 9:10-17)*. And I had the reassurance that Jesus would always be with me *(Matthew 28:20)*.

◆◆◆

The enemy also attacked me with Scripture. He asked how I could possibly think writing could be okay, because the Bible said *"'Honor your father and mother'—which is the first commandment with a promise—'so that it may go well with you and that you may enjoy long life on the earth'"* (Ephesians 6:2). Clearly sharing so much painful history would be dishonoring my parents.

That was a lie that God took care of in three ways. First, He had the Spirit prompt me to meet with my mom in the fall of 2019.

I was extremely nervous to talk to my mom about the journey God had me on. I had no idea what to expect. But as we sat alone in my kitchen, Mom told me that she thought it would be wonderful for me to help other women. (I had told her some of how hard things had been lately; that God had helped me; and that He had led me to want to write and speak.)

Mom told me to do whatever it took to get well. She told me that she admired my teaching abilities and thought I'd be a good speaker and writer. She even asked if I needed anything from her. And she understood I wasn't operating from a place of anger, but from a place of loving God and being obedient. Her response lifted an enormous weight off of me.

Second, God had me meet with Dad (and Mom and Will) at the beginning of December 2019. I told my dad that I wasn't keeping the past private anymore—not because I was angry at him, but because I needed to help other women just as I had been helped. I told him that I had been getting treatment for PTSD, which had been hard, and that I was doing better.

I brought up positive things he had done over the years and told him I could see how much he had done in my adult life to be a good father. I also let him know how much it meant to me that he had been the one family member to attend my baptism years ago, even though he wasn't a believer. And I reiterated that Jesus was for my dad too; that it would be my dearest wish for him to accept Christ and I would never stop praying for that. To be totally transparent, I let him know that

Daniel now knew about the past. I told him that Daniel was still processing it, but that he knew that Grandpa had been nothing but good to him his whole life. That he loved him.

And I let my Dad know I wasn't looking for our relationship to end. I asked if I could hug him, and he said yes. So I did. As we hugged, I asked if he had any questions for me about what I was going to do, and he shook his head no. And praise God, we parted that day on good terms.

My mom sent me a text an hour later saying she knew that had been hard for me. And that she loved me very much.

It was hard, but it was also a liberating experience! God chose to make a way where the enemy said it was impossible. As I stepped out in obedience, God stood with me and protected me.

But God also followed up by helping me understand the distortion in the enemy's use of Scripture. God's command to honor my father and mother was intended to have me recognize the authority He gives to parents, not to elevate any authority over His own.

Jesus said, *"Anyone who loves his father or mother more than Me is not worthy of Me; anyone who loves his son or daughter more than Me is not worthy of Me; and anyone who does not take up his cross and follow Me is not worthy of Me. Whoever finds his life will lose it, and whoever loses his life for My sake will find it"* (Matthew 10:37-39 BSB).

EVEN IF my parents hadn't reacted well it would still have been right to follow God's plan for writing this book. And EVEN IF trouble crops up later in our relationship because of my obedience, I have His promise that *"goodness and mercy will follow me all the days of my life, and I will dwell in the house of the LORD forever"* (Psalm 23:6 BSB).

◆◆◆

And that brings me to my only child—my son, Daniel. I praise God with all my heart for the goodness and mercy that follows me there.

Let me start by saying that in no way does our son think my husband and I are perfect. He has seen us mess up repeatedly over the years. But thanks be to God, he's seen more than that.

Instead, my son's first reaction when I told him my story (in addition to shock) was to let me know what a powerful testimony for God it was. We talked at length. And then he started sorting through his feelings with a counselor.

Not only has my previous witness not been damaged, but Daniel—after seeking my permission, which was an amazing event for me—incorporated my story into his own testimony. He told me he needed to tell other people about what God has done to redeem our family—both the marriage being put back together and my childhood history. He said it's a big part of why he believes what he does.

And as far as Grandpa goes: Daniel had already been praying for his salvation, and he is continuing. He loves him and would celebrate that victory!

Does your legacy matter to you?

◆◆◆

A beautiful thing happened last year on our wedding anniversary. It was the first year we got to celebrate where Daniel was fully informed of family history.

As a present, he surprised me and Will with a letter that took our breath away. I found it incredibly healing to receive! And it continues to give me great peace and hope about our legacy.

◆◆◆

November 13, 2019

Dear Mom and Dad,

    Happy Anniversary! I am so happy that I get to celebrate your inspiring and God-filled marriage today. I thought a good way to celebrate would be to tell you what I see when I look at you both.
    When I look at your marriage, the first thing I see is two people who honor each other and others. As God has used your marriage to strengthen you both and grow you closer to Him, so He has also used you in many ways to touch the lives of those around you. Everyone I have ever met who has come into contact with you two has told me about how kind, loving, and respectful you both are and how glad they are to know you. God has used you both together to encourage and help so many people who need it, and I am so proud of how much you both choose to honor and follow Him in all that you do.
    When I look at your marriage, I also see two people not just in love, but who choose to love each other each day, no matter how hard it gets. Through thick and thin, through good and bad, your decision and commitment to love and support each other has been a blessing to others and a foundation for me as I've grown up. By prioritizing your relationship and showing me that your love for God and for each other were the most important things in our house, you showed me what a healthy marriage looks like and gave me a safe and secure home in which to grow and become who God made me to be. For that I am more thankful than I can ever express.
    Finally, when I look at your marriage, I see the value of facing life together rather than going it alone. As you both help, refine, and support each other through each stage of life, I am continually reminded that life is better when it is lived with people you trust and who trust you. And, as you both extend that love, support, and encouragement to me, I am blessed to have you both as much-needed lights and signposts pointing back to Jesus during my darkest moments. I love you both more than I can ever say, and I am blessed beyond measure to know, without any doubt, that you both love me more than you can ever say as well.

Thank you both for all that you do and for all that you put on display. Again, Happy Anniversary!
   Love, Daniel

◆◆◆

As I was getting close to finishing this book, I had a dream. It was like a dream I'd had some time before, but different.

The first time I had dreamed that I stood in a spotlight surrounded by terrifying creatures. They kept lunging at me and hissing something so menacing that I shook where I stood.

Then I realized I wasn't in a spotlight. Jesus was there, shining like nothing I'd ever seen. He was standing in front of me on every side, somehow, gently encouraging me to raise my head. He told me that I wasn't in danger. None of what I was surrounded by could get through Him.

So I raised my head. And the creatures howled. They recognized the truth of what He said, and they were furious. They redoubled their attack, but it didn't matter. They could have destroyed me in an instant, except for my Shield. Jesus was impervious to their attack.

But He wasn't impervious to me. He was open. I've never felt so connected and loved.

When I had the dream again recently, it had changed. I was still standing surrounded by those creatures, and a light was shining. But this time I couldn't see Jesus. And I was afraid.

I wondered where He was—there was still so much light. And then I realized the light was coming from inside me. The Spirit of God was present whether I could see Jesus or not. I just had to recognize that and let my faith be bigger than my fear.

At that realization, I woke up with a start, rolled over, and slipped my hand into my husband's hand. He didn't fully wake up, but gently returned my squeeze.

A peace swept over me. So much had changed! The walk through the valley had been worth it. Though there would be trouble in this life, Christ had overcome it *(John 16:33)*; and in Him, I could walk forward, goodness and mercy following me, loving others out of the overflow of being loved. Thanks be to God; my eyes were open! And my heart was truly happy.

AUTHOR'S CONCLUSION: LETTER TO MY DAD

"If you confess with your mouth, 'Jesus is Lord,' and believe in your heart that God raised Him from the dead, you will be saved." Romans 10:9 BSB

◆◆◆

There is a lot of sharing about past sexual abuse going on in our culture right now. And I am hopeful that the Light shining into darkness *(John 1:5)* will help many people.

While I am NOT advocating that all survivors reach out to their abusers, which would be dangerous in many instances, I AM advocating forgiveness, and that the Christian community as a whole open their eyes to see that both the survivors of and perpetrators of abuse are God's children in need of healing.

Justice is good. Justice is desirable! But vengeance belongs to the Lord. Be very wary of any cultural movement that claims that healing comes from revenge. It does not.

"Do not avenge yourselves, beloved, but leave room for God's wrath. For it is written: 'Vengeance is Mine; I will repay, says the Lord.' On the contrary, if your enemy is hungry, feed him; if he is thirsty, give him a drink. For in so doing, you will heap burning coals on his head.' Do not be overcome by evil, but overcome evil with good." (Romans 12:19-21 BSB)

The light God gave me to shine *(Luke 8:16-18)* is His truth that nothing that anyone has done is beyond the healing power of the blood of Jesus. God loves people on both sides of trauma. As Scripture says, *"For God so loved the world that He gave His one and only Son, that everyone who believes in Him shall not perish but have eternal life. For God did not send His Son into the world to condemn the world, but to save the world through Him. Whoever believes in Him is not condemned, but whoever does not believe has already been condemned, because he has not believed in the name of God's one and only Son" (John 3:16-18 BSB).* Salvation is for EVERYONE who accepts Jesus as Lord. And on that note...

◆◆◆

Dear Dad,

You're right that the story we leave behind here is our legacy. And a huge part of your story is represented by your children: who you are with your children matters; what you teach your children matters; and how you treat your children's children matters.

You've done many things already to repair your legacy. Throughout my adult life, you have been a very good father. But there's something bigger at stake here than that story. Because eternity is real. Salvation or condemnation is real. Your story doesn't stop with your death: you either go to Heaven or you go to Hell.

I understand how hard it is to take a leap of faith. I found it incredibly difficult myself. But I can promise you without reservation that God and Jesus are completely worth it. And you are wanted in Heaven! Both by God and by me.

You don't have to understand everything before you pray to accept Christ—and you don't have to feel some supernatural connection first. When you ask Jesus to forgive you and start leading your life, He will absolutely do that. You can count on it.

With our story in the light, you have the opportunity to leave an amazing legacy: a story of God's love and redeeming power that will reach far beyond our family. The best legacy you could ever leave would be the knowledge that our story, fully redeemed by God, would continue in Heaven. Because God's love is just that big. That's reality also.

I love you no matter what! And I'm still praying for you.
Your daughter,
Carolyn

AFTERWORD: ON FORGIVENESS AND FREEDOM BY CHARLES SPEER

◆◆◆

The deeper the hurt, the more profound is the healing. How do we go from crippling fear and bitterness to forgiveness and freedom? Only in Jesus Christ is it possible.

As a prison ministry volunteer, I see many who were victims of sexual abuse become abusers themselves. Imagine the shame and guilt commonly experienced by victims compounded by the shame and guilt of the offender. Add to that the loathing and rejection of friends, family, and society at large. It is no wonder that many will come out of incarceration more bitter than before and likely to reoffend.

Sex crimes carry such stigma that many offenders cannot face squarely their responsibility for their actions. As a former homicide/sex crimes detective, I was amazed that men would readily admit to murder and yet deny the rape that preceded the death of the victim. How are we then ever able to break the cycle of abuse that so devastates families of every class and race?

Carolyn found the answer. Jesus heals and forgives! As she received healing, she extended that same grace to those who perpetrated horrific abuse against her. It may sound simple and easy, but it isn't. It is messy and follows a torturous path because we are messy and deceived by Satan's lies.

Carolyn has asked that her story be shared with incarcerated offenders in the hope that in the grace of God they would receive healing and forgiveness. She is living out the grace and love that Jesus displayed on the cross. No greater story can ever be told!

Charles Speer
Paul and Silas Prison Ministries
PO Box 46533 | Little Rock, AR 72204
facebook.com/PaulandSilasPM

AUTHOR'S THANK YOU

◆◆◆

I started this journey afraid to talk to anyone and was blessed by more people who wanted to listen than I could ever have imagined.

To my therapist, Rosemary, who is clearly called by God to be doing what she does: thank you, thank you, thank you!

To my sweet husband Will, and my son Daniel, who lightened my load the entire time I healed and wrote this book: you are amazing! God blessed me beyond measure when He gave me you.

To my mom, who helped rebuild my heart by encouraging me to do whatever it took to heal: I love you, Mom!

To my many praying friends—most especially Shannon and Jan, who proved able to take ANYTHING in stride on a daily basis—thank you for standing in the gap and fighting for me!

To my sweet Jamie, whose patience for reading and re-reading is incredible: thank you for having my back 100%! For tons of editing! For all the prayer and all the love! You rock, sister!

To my other draft readers who were all so kind and encouraging (including Jennifer P., who opted to let me live and continue writing...she really hates "to be continued"), thank you so much!

To Samantha and Wendy, who formed a focus group and tried out all the questions: I love you more than you know!

To Pastor Will Stevens and Charles Speer: thank you for walking with me and giving me insight that I could never have gained without you!

To Louise Allison, who shines for Christ and encourages me to do the same: thank you, thank you, thank you!

To Pastor Mark Evans, who saved me from complete meltdowns by providing practical action steps—both spiritual and writing-related—on multiple occasions: God bless you! Your patience and your insight are truly remarkable.

To Pastor Greg Kirksey, who let God use him as a catalyst, a teacher, a big brother and a prayer warrior throughout this journey: I could not be more grateful for all the love and support!

To Pastor Jason Curry, whose lessons on evangelism are exceptional: thank you for modeling what truth in love looks like. Your coaching gave me confidence!

To Pastor Russ Holmes, who sent us on our re|engage journey—I'm more grateful than you know!

To my couples life group, Shook 'N Crew; my women's life group, "The Sweet Church Ladies"; and all of my friends in Women Equipped: you could not have been more supportive! Thank you so very much.

And to Christine Caine, who doesn't know me at all, but whose devotionals in my email inbox helped me over some pretty rough bumps: God bless you!!

To God be the glory! In the mighty name of Jesus. Amen.

CHAPTER DISCUSSION QUESTIONS

◆◆◆

Chapter 1

Did you know that the Hebrew word for "blessed" was the same as the word for "happy"? When you think about happiness, are you thinking about worldly happiness—happiness based on what's happening—or holy happiness?

Have you ever had a major life interruption where all you could do was rely on god to get through everyday tasks? What did that look like? How did you lean on god, and what was the result?

When you're angry, how do you deal with it? And does that improve the situation, leave it the same, or make it worse?

Chapter 2

Patterns and consequences of sin do travel down generational lines. But it is possible to break that cycle. Are there any stories in your own family where you need a victory from God? Or where you have seen a victory happen that you want to share?

Where is your value rooted? Is your sense of self easily rocked by positive and negative feedback?

Do you have any big "WHY" questions for God about anything you've lived through?

Chapter 3

Does life change scare you? Do you cling to "functioning in your dysfunction"? Is your "normal" an idol?

There are a lot of misconceptions about forgiveness covered in Chapter 3. Did any of them challenge you? Is there any area of your life where you should be extending forgiveness?

Have you ever heard someone else's testimony and been moved to action? Have you ever shared your own testimony and seen God use it?

Chapter 4

Do you believe God cares about the pain His children are in?

Do you have any unhealed pain?

Do you see any connection between unhealed pain and the struggle with God for control over life?

Chapter 5

It doesn't take major trauma to leave scars on a person's spirit. Do you ever struggle with anxiety or depression?

Have you ever thought about God designing our brains to heal the same way he designed our skin to heal?

Could therapy resources address a need you have in your own life (feeling safe, control over overwhelming thoughts, or identifying feelings)?

Chapter 6

How big is your God?

Have you ever felt despair? What got you through?

What are you willing to give Jesus?

Chapter 7

Have you ever used Scripture to fight your battles? What verses have been meaningful to you?

Do you have an accountability partner (or any safe person) to share your struggles with?

What do you meditate on? What is your "hosos" (whatever)? Is it God-sized and God-honoring?

Chapter 8

Did you know that the point of marriage was to grow toward Christ-likeness together?

Does your spouse know what areas you struggle in? Do you know what areas your spouse struggles in?

What could God do with you as a couple if you trusted Him to lead your relationship? Or if You are letting Him lead you as a couple, what have you seen Him do?

Chapter 9

Do you have a God-story you need to share but haven't? What holds you back?

Has the enemy ever tried to misconstrue Scripture to hold you back from God's plan for you?

What legacy would you like to leave in this world?

CELEBRATE RECOVERY

◆◆◆

Is Celebrate Recovery for you or someone you know?

Are you or someone you know struggling with...

- Addiction
- Anger
- Codependency
- Eating Disorder
- Food Addiction
- Love & Relationship Addiction
- Physical/Sexual/Emotional Abuse
- Alcohol/Drug Addiction
- Sexual Addiction
- Gambling Addiction

Celebrate Recovery is a "large umbrella" 12 Step Program to help a limitless number of issues.

It is a biblical and balanced program effective in helping people overcome their hurts, hang-ups and habits.

Find a group near you:

http://locator.crgroups.info/

celebraterecovery.com

PARTNERS AGAINST TRAFFICKING HUMANS

◆◆◆

PATH advocates for those victimized by the sex-industry by providing a safe environment where healing can occur, making success possible and dreams achievable.

PATH+ is a program specifically designed to care for survivor-offenders.

PATH
PARTNERS AGAINST TRAFFICKING HUMANS

Campus PATH is working with colleges and universities state-wide to establish and maintain anti-trafficking groups on every campus in Arkansas.

Help us help them! Donate now!
pathsaves.networkforgood.com/projects/67793-general-fund

Partners Against Trafficking Humans
P.O. Box 21066 | Little Rock, Arkansas 72221
pathsaves.org | info@pathsaves.org
Main Phone: 501.993.1641
Victim's Services: 501.301.4357
U.S. National Hotline: 1.888.373.7888

THE CHURCH AT ROCK CREEK

◆◆◆

WATCH ROCK CREEK SERVICES ONLINE!

TWITTER
twitter.com/rockcreektweet

FACEBOOK
facebook.com/thechurchatrockcreek

WEBSITE
churchatrockcreek.com/media/live

GIVE ONLINE:
Ministry at Rock Creek never stops! Every week we are able to reach people with the message of God's love because of your generosity. Visit our web site (churchatrockcreek.com/give) to learn more about all the ways you can give today!

THE CHURCH AT
ROCK CREEK

11500 West 36th Street
Little Rock, AR 72211
1-501-225-8684
info@churchatrockcreek.com
Mark Evans, Senior Pastor

Made in the USA
Middletown, DE
09 February 2024